SILENT NO MORE

HEALING FROM WORKPLACE BULLYING

BY ELIZABETH GRAY

First published in 2021 by Elizabeth Gray

© Elizabeth Gray
The moral rights of the author have been asserted.
This book is a SpiritCast Network of Books

Author:

Gray, Elizabeth

Title:

Silent No More; Healing from Workplace Bullying

ISBN:

978-1-71649-695-0

All rights reserved. Except as permitted under the Australian Copyright Act 1968 (for example, a fair dealing for the purposes of study, research, criticism or review), no part of this book may be reproduced, stored in a retrieval system, communicated or transmitted in any form or by any means without prior written permission. All enquiries should be made to the author at liz_g@bigpond.com

Editor-in-chief: Anita Saunders
Cover Design: Sarah Rose Graphic Design

Scripture quotations taken from The Holy Bible, New International Version® NIV®

Copyright © 1973 1978 1984 2011 by Biblica, Inc.™ Used by permission. All rights reserved worldwide.

Disclaimer:

The material in this publication is of the nature of general comment only and does not represent professional advice. It is not intended to provide specific guidance for particular circumstances, and it should not be relied on as the basis for any decision to take action or not take action on any matter which it covers. Readers should obtain professional advice where appropriate, before making any such decision. To the maximum extent permitted by law, the author and publisher disclaim all responsibility and liability to any person, arising directly or indirectly from any person taking or not taking action based on the information in this publication.

TABLE OF CONTENTS

Disclaimer .... *ix*
    Trigger Warning...ix

Dedication .... *xi*

Part One—Me **1**
    Silent No More 2
    A little about me and my journey 5
    In God's Hand 13

Introduction *15*
    Why I wrote this book 15
    Hiding in the Shadows 21

Chapter 1—Choosing myself *23*
    Owning all of me 24
    Dealing with bullying behaviour 26
    Why choosing yourself is important and not selfish 29
    You are not broken 30
    It is okay to be you, and you matter 31
    The Gems Within 34

Chapter 2—Societal Expectations *35*
    What is expected of us? 36
    Being defined 38
    Other people's messages 38
    Playing small 40
    Staying safe 40
    Deep Wounds 43

Chapter 3—Highly Sensitive Person and Empaths ... 45
- Highly sensitive person 46
- Empath 47
- Paranoia 49
- Intuition and red flags 50
- Listen to the Heart 54

Part Two—Bullying 55
- Gaslighting 56

Chapter 4—Bullying, Narcissistic, and Gaslighting Behaviour 57
- Bullying behaviour 58
- Narcissistic behaviour 59
- Narcissistic supply 60
- False self 61
- Gaslighting behaviour 62
- What are the characteristics you have that narcissists target? 65
- Relationships with empaths 67
- Silenced 68

Chapter 5—Psychological Safety, Misuse of Power, Toxic Workplaces 69
- Psychological safety 70
- Misuse of power 71
- Victim blaming 74
- Toxic workplaces 76
- Being in the Light 79

Chapter 6—Being Bullied 81
- Shame 90
- Writing a new story 90
- Standing on the Edge 93

Chapter 7—Impacts of Bullying *95*
    Anger and bitterness... 96
    Financial, mental, and physical health................................ 98
    The after-effects... 99
    Past, Present, Future.. 108

Chapter 8—Justice/Redress *109*
    Talking to management about the issues........................ 112
    Non-disclosure agreements 113
    Burnout... 113
    The cut has been so deep... 115

Part Three—Fear, Courage, and God 117
    The Dark Storms 118

Chapter 9—Fear/Courage, Grief,
    Anxiety, and Depression *119*
    Remaining silent.. 120
    Facing fear and the unknown.. 120
    Dealing with fear 121
    Courage... 124
    Grief... 125
    Anxiety and depression.. 126
    Suicide... 128
    I Am Here... 131

Chapter 10—Faith and God-Directed Purpose . *133*
    Ephesians 6: The Armor of God 139

Part Four—Learning From the Experiences .143
    The Knowing.. 144

Chapter 11—My Healing *145*
    Things We Can Do 150

Chapter 12—What Worked for Me 151
Inner Work 158

Chapter 13—Doing the Inner Work 159
Be your own best friend 164
Awareness 164
Expecting others to change 164
Healing our wounds and suffering 165
Emotions/triggers/resilience 166
Releasing our emotions 168
No judgement/complaining 169
Shadow self 170
Taking back your power 173
Boundaries 174
Boundaries and people with toxic behaviour 176
Learning to face obstacles and challenges 177
Belief 177
Little steps 179
Life after 182

Chapter 14—Learning From Experiences 183
Reality vs future 185
Being grateful 187
Asking for help and what I needed 188
Giving and receiving 189
Resilience 190
Healing Myself 194

Chapter 15—How We Know When We Are Healed 195
Counteracting bullying 197

Part Five—Life After Bullying 199
    Finding My Voice 200

Chapter 16—Big Dreams and Life After Bullying 201
    Finding your voice 204
    Divine purpose listening to your
        soul and the messages 205
    Doing the things for yourself that you love 206
    Find your tribe 206
    Moving into the future ensuring no repeating 207
    Contribution forward 207
    Dream big 209
    Be committed 209
    Keep promises to yourself 210
    One Wild and Precious Life 212

Conclusion 213
    One Wild and Precious Life 214

Part Six—References and Help 217
    Remaining Open 218

Workplace Bullying—What Employers Need to Do 219
    How do you want your employees to feel? 221
    Factors that contribute to workplace bullying 221
    Speaking up 222
    Feedback 223
    Toxicity damage to companies 224
    Employees feeling psychological safety 226
    Win/win 228

Exercises to Help Healing 231

Resources... *237*
    Contacts for anxiety and depression.................. 238
    Resources around narcissism............................. 238
    Books 239
    Prayer 239

About the Author *241*

Thank you... *243*

DISCLAIMER

This is my story and I have written it from my heart and how I felt undergoing these experiences.

Trigger Warning

The content of this book goes deep into incidents that happened to me around bullying, narcissist behaviour, and gaslighting and some of these may trigger you and bring back unwanted memories and emotions.

Please do not hesitate to seek professional help if you need it.

DEDICATION

It is only in our darkest hours that we may discover the true strength of the brilliant light within ourselves that can never, ever be dimmed—Doe Zantamata.

This book is dedicated to those who have suffered from bullying, narcissistic abuse, and gaslighting in the workplace, and from anxiety and depression. You are all precious, loved, worthy, and you matter. There is no mistake that you are in this world. You have so much to offer, and your voice and story is needed by others. I salute your bravery in acknowledging these issues and working through them. I truly hope that you will find something in this book to help you heal and find the wonderful light within you and never allow it to be dimmed.

Thanks to God for the small whispers, nudges, and the challenges that have led me to write this book and follow the path to healing. Over many years, God has given me so many blessings and taken care of me and kept me sane through some very difficult periods in my life. I am so grateful for those dark patches as they have enabled me to grow, and I am proud of my journey and who I am.

Thanks to my parents, Beryl and Bill Gray, who are looking on from heaven, and to my brother Andrew, his wife Kathy, my nieces Samantha and Sascha, and to my four-legged nephew Ollie.

To my colleagues who have suffered bullying, narcissistic abuse, and gaslighting behaviours with me, thanks for all your support and letting me know I was not alone in my journey.

Silent No More

To my many wonderful friends (the list is long) who have stuck with me through the adversity, thanks for listening to me and encouraging me. Thanks for adding the joy of your friendship into my life. I would not have made it through without you.

Part One
Me

*I am allowed to be me and you don't define
me, my voice, thoughts, or feelings
– Elizabeth Gray*

Silent No More

The birds can sing with their voice
But I am told to be silent
A baby cries when hungry or in discomfort
But I am told to be silent
A whale can sing a song metres below the ocean
But I am told to be silent
Other people can talk and sing
But I am told to be silent
Noise can be everywhere
But I am told to be silent

Why won't you see me?
Why won't you hear me?
Why don't you want to understand me?

I am about to explode

Why did you decide I am irrelevant?
Why did you decide I don't matter?
Why did you decide you had control over me?
Why did you decide you were more important than me?

But I have a small voice getting louder and louder

I matter
I am a gift from God and God does not make mistakes

I will not be silent anymore
To be silent means I will be sick and unhealthy

Elizabeth Gray

No, not anymore
I will not be silent
I am allowed to express my thoughts and feelings
Why do you think that is irrelevant?

I am allowed to be me and you don't define me, my voice, thoughts, or feelings

I matter
I choose me!!!

Elizabeth Gray 2020

PREFACE

*The gem cannot be polished without friction,
no man perfected without trials*
—Chinese Proverb.

A little about me and my journey

This book is about my journey healing from workplace bullying but before I go ahead, I want to share my background so you can understand how I got to that place.

For many years, I listened to other people on what they thought of me and how I should live my life. I also believed life was happening to me rather than for me. My continual focus was on the negatives in my life rather than the positives. I became a complainer and could not find myself out of the maze I was hopelessly lost in. I suffered from a major depression 20 years ago and seriously considered committing suicide as life was too tough and unenjoyable to live. Suddenly this was lifted by God as a wonderful miracle and I did not go into those deep depths again, but occasionally suffer from depression.

I bought lots of self-development books and went to psychologists seeking help. Some of the self-development is that message that you are broken but you are really not broken. You don't have to fix yourself but change your mind, beliefs, identities, and habits. Fear was a constant companion in my life: fear of success, fear of failure, fear of being laughed at (this was an old wound from my childhood). I read and understood but what I lacked was taking action and trying things irrespective of results. I did not believe that good things could happen to me, or I was worthy of good things. These beliefs really held me back from living an enjoyable life. I felt miserable and I found it hard to enjoy my life.

I did study art at TAFE and really enjoyed the creative journey. However, I find it hard to prioritise doing the things that give me joy in my life. One of the ways I started to do this was by learning how to quilt and made some really good friends through this. I have taken a few trips overseas to places I always dreamed of going to, including India, the Taj Mahal, and the pyramids in Egypt. Over time, I found that my enjoyment from work was getting less and less as I did not feel completely fulfilled. In my work, the times I had enjoyed were around training other people and helping them. I was too afraid to believe that I could do work doing something I loved. I loved all the quotes from people regarding doing what you love and thought this is for other people and not me.

For me growing up, the usual track was going to school, going to university, getting a job, getting married, having children, buying a house, retiring at a specific age. There was nothing about being an entrepreneur. You kept risk-taking to a minimum and looked up to authority figures as being Gods and that they knew best. I was raised by parents who both lost homes during their childhood, one through separation of a marriage and the other through economic circumstances. Both of their losses impacted on the way they looked at the world and how I looked at the world in having a safe job and being employed.

As a single woman not married or having children, I struggled with this. This is very much a hidden pain among women that is not widely shared with others. Too often an assumption is made about you and what you choose in your life. Sometimes life happens to you and things don't work out how you planned, and it is sad as you wished and dreamed about something else.

Elizabeth Gray

I spent many years of my childhood being bullied for how I looked and who I was. All this time, I did not realise I had a light shining in me and I allowed this light to be dimmed because of other people. I am kind and giving and did not have good boundaries. Boundaries are rules we put around other people's behaviour in our lives. This means not tolerating their bad behaviour and letting them know. I did not think myself worthy or loved myself in any way. I so wanted to be loved and I sacrificed myself for others and became a people pleaser. This ultimately attracted the wrong kind of people in that they were dominating and wanting to take and take from me as it was about them and not me.

Often in our childhood before the age of seven, something happens, and we interpret it and develop coping mechanisms and behaviours to help us through life. I know my parents loved me but somehow, I developed a way of coping that did not serve me through my life. I have allowed others to dominate me, especially if they had a dominant personality. I had trouble saying no and had not been taught to say no. Throughout my life I suffered a lot of health issues during different times. When your body is sick it is much harder to stand up for yourself.

I have learned that the body gives us information and tells us about unhealthy situations, but we don't often know how to listen. Listening to the silent whispers are important and what messages you get from other people. Other people do reveal to you what they are like. I am an empath and I feel so much of other people's energy, and I did not know how to deal with it. I had to learn that it was not mine to take on.

I was conditioned as a young girl that other people were to come before me, and I was the last one to be considered. This created a belief that I was responsible for other people's reactions to me. So, if they were upset with me, it was my fault instead of me knowing that I needed to put in a boundary. Quite often, when I did put in a boundary and people did not like it, they were upset. Many girls were taught the way of putting others first and themselves last. Thankfully things are slowly changing for the better and self-care is important for women.

I have been on a lifetime journey to grow and live a life of joy. What changed for me? I ended leaving a job due to constant bullying and someone being out to get me as I was a threat to their need to be adored and in control. This was very difficult to deal with as this shook me to the very core of my being. I believed what they said about me was true. The information coming to me was not from a healthy individual but the opposite. I was isolated by the team and I had people turned against me. I was also told by my psychologist that I was the biggest bully to myself. How true was this? Very true; I had put high standards on myself and constantly thought of myself as a failure and spoke to myself harshly and put myself down all the time. I was so negative about myself. We would never treat our friends like that or allow that behaviour towards our friends, so why do we allow it for ourselves? We should not; we need to be our own best friends and treat ourselves well.

I had often focused on the negative and Tony Robbins' quote helped me focus on what could go right instead of looking constantly at what could go wrong.

> ***Stop being afraid of what could go wrong, and start being excited of what could go right**—Tony Robbins.*

Elizabeth Gray

One of the things that opened my eyes to changing my mindset and being coached was that I went to a seminar called "Prosper From Your Passion" by Ben Harvey from Authentic Education. I subsequently enrolled in a few of their courses. I found a lot of healing through their Accelerated Coaching Certification course. I did not heal overnight but my change journey had begun. It took another three years and three coaches to help me along my way to where I love and accept myself; I have self-worth. It took even more time to accept my body even though I loved myself.

Leaving another job just as COVID-19 came along allowed me to spend time at home and continue to heal myself from the many years of scars from workplace bullying and the childhood wounds I was carrying. I conquered some of my fear in regard to leaving and creating a new life for myself and removing the traditional way of thinking that I needed a job to make me whole. During this time, I chose myself over others. I was exhausted from giving and not feeling fulfilled by my work.

Another course, "Made To Do This" by Cathy Heller, which I started in January 2020, really helped twist my mind into being an entrepreneur and enjoying my life and seeking to find joy in my work. The idea of being messy and imperfect as well as keeping on going and pivoting was so refreshing. The support from my accountability group was amazing and truly one of the greatest blessings from the course. One thing I learned was about taking action and doing things in the face of fear, i.e., 20 seconds of courage from the book *We Bought a Zoo*.

Everyone is different; these are things that worked for me. Your journey may be different, and it might be a coach or another course that helps you. You will need to tailor it, so it works for you. I also started to write poetry, and this really helped me to release what I was feeling. I would write what I thought on the day.

I decided that I matter, and I am here on earth with a mission from God. It is not selfish to choose me and I needed to be in alignment with God and my purpose. I have previously tolerated so much abuse in my life from other people and myself, which was not healthy. In choosing me, it is not about ignoring others or their needs. It is about making myself whole and healthy so I can serve people filled up instead of being in an empty place. It is about doing things I love while helping others. This journey will continue but I am grateful that I have chosen myself like God chose me.

The answers for myself were always in me but I was looking externally instead of internally. God whispers into our hearts but often due to our beliefs we don't listen. God will guide us but when we continually ignore what he has put into our hearts, experiences and obstacles come our way until we listen. I call my experience with a particular workplace as like being hit by a Mack truck. Pain is a wakeup call that there is something happening that you need to address. I am so grateful for the experience as it confirmed to me that I did not deserve these experiences and I needed to dig deeper into myself in order to heal. All experiences in life will have positives and negatives.

When an event has happened to us, based on our experiences and knowledge at the time, we create a meaning to this event and it turns into a story that we tell ourselves. It is these stories that influence how we see the circumstances in our lives. Having negative experiences can able us to grow and can propel us forward. The contrast between negative and positive experiences helps us see what we have in our life to be grateful for.

Having emotions is normal but it is how we deal with them that is very important. Dealing with your emotions in a healthy way will help you get through difficult times. To process emotions means you need to feel the emotions (not avoid them), and this can be done by sitting with the emotions and allow yourself to feel them. It is then easier to let them go. Never allow other people to dictate what your emotions are and how you should feel.

Find people who will actually listen to and be empathetic with you. Stick with those people who encourage you and support you and want the very best for you. No one else is living your life so don't tolerate those who don't want the best for you. Choose yourself. See the possibilities in your life to grow and have joy. Life won't be without obstacles and challenges, but you will see them as a way to move forward rather than stop you.

Trust that the universe has a bigger, wider, deeper dream for you than you could ever imagine for yourself—Oprah Winfrey.

In God's Hand

My heart kept whispering to me
I had so little faith and belief in myself
So I ignored the whispering
I kept on working and doing what I knew how
The unhappiness and ill health continued
Deep down within my soul it knew
But I had so much fear and lacked the courage to listen
The whispering became a roar
That I could not ignore
Circumstances were happening that were out of my control
But God's hand was with me
Rescuing me from a bad situation
Renewing my heart and belief in myself
Inspiring and leading me on the journey
That God has prepared me for
Allowing me to grow and face my challenges
All by giving me so much grace and mercy
So safe within God's hands
Which I am eternally grateful for

Elizabeth Gray 2020

INTRODUCTION

In the hero's journey, the heroes need villains just as much as villains need heroes. The challenges from trials and rivals make us grow and become better. The power and strength of the villain determines the necessary power and strength of the hero. If the villain is weak, there would be nothing to vanquish—and no need for the hero to rise to greatness
—Jim Kwik.

Why I wrote this book

I began to write this book to tell my story of what happened to me from many years of workplace bullying and to help me heal from the abuse I suffered. Healing is an ongoing journey for me. For my health, I needed to express my voice and no longer be silent about the things that happened. My hope with this book is that it will take you on the path of healing and finding your voice. We all have the power to change our lives by creating our own future and leaving behind the past.

I look back on my journey and see my growth and I am proud of myself for what I did and for standing up throughout this book and saying a **big NO to bullying, narcissistic abuse, and gaslighting behaviour in the workplace.** This type of behaviour in the workplace has to stop as usually the victim/survivor loses out and the one with the bullying behaviour wins. If I can help one person who was in a similar situation to myself, this book will be well worth it. A lot of things happen in silence, and it is not until we are brave and speak up, that things begin to change.

There is an enormous silence around workplace bullying and there are huge financial, mental, and physical impacts to the victim/survivor. To prove bullying places a heavy burden on the victim/survivor, and they are often not listened to or believed. Also, those with bullying behaviour have considerable experience in this behaviour and are well versed with manipulating the situation as well as placing fear in the victim/survivor. Another silence that affects the victim/survivor is in regard to future employment: to obtain a reference from the employer, the victim/survivor has to play nice and leave on good terms and then is unable to mention what happened to them to future employers/employment agencies due to the standard approach of not disparaging your previous employer. This means that bullying remains partially unknown in the employment market and continues in the workplace. In the past, I used to follow that track and kept any comments to the minimum so I could gain further employment.

I have found by documenting my journey of healing from the unhealthy patterns in my life around bullying behaviour I have grown and have incredible hope for the future. I trust that this book may be of inspiration to those who have been through a similar experience or anybody who knows someone going through this experience. These types of experiences can be completely devastating to the victims as often the attacks are quite personal and strike at the heart of the victim's soul. It is not a matter of telling someone to leave their workplace, get over it, and move on. People need to be able to heal from the experience and this takes time. Unfortunately, in some cases, people do not recover from being at the receiving end of these types of behaviours.

Elizabeth Gray

Anyone can be a victim of bullying and narcissistic behaviour. Often the people targeted are kind, helpful, giving, empathetic, reliable, and excellent at their job. The person with the narcissistic and bullying behaviour has no boundaries, like the victim, making it a match in hell for the victim. The person with the bullying behaviour often is projecting their insecurities onto the victim/survivor.

For myself, I had very few boundaries in my personal and business life, and I kept attracting people with no boundaries into my life. I certainly did not deserve the treatment I endured from their behaviour. This pattern was consistent in my life where I gave and gave to others to get recognition, validation, and was a people pleaser. Despite the pain from others' behaviour, I still gave and gave, and suffering became my new normal. From these experiences, I needed to recognise what was not working in my life. I needed to heal myself, to love myself, see my own self-worth, and put in boundaries that their behaviour was unacceptable. I found this easier to do in my personal life than I did in my professional life at work.

I had to identify where my childhood wounds were as these are the ones bullies can see and tap into. These wounds were of not feeling worthy, not feeling loved, and not feeling good enough. For me, it was important to heal myself from these childhood wounds and enforce my boundaries and speak up. Unless we speak up, we are telling people how to treat us when we accept bad behaviour from them. We need to speak up and not be afraid or be silenced and tell them, this behaviour is unacceptable.

My priority was healing myself from the bullying, both mental and physically. I certainly did not want to put myself back into that position again to be targeted by bullying in the workplace and I have chosen that I am not accepting that in my life anymore. Writing this book, finding myself and my voice, and knowing I matter was paramount. Looking back over my life, in my need to have recognition and significance, I was ignoring my purpose and being who I was meant to be. It is sad that we don't listen to our inner voices, and we allow others to drown our voice out. The message from our soul starts with a whisper and then gets louder and louder until it hits us hard. One particular experience was so intense but also the message from God was there. It is time to take up your purpose and for me that is writing and art. It was time to be myself and no-one else.

Courage is what takes you out of there. Finding the courage to say no, having the courage to leave a job or relationship with toxic behaviour. You were meant for much more. The experience you have undergone can be very traumatic and the healing begins within you, inside. Be all of yourself. God created an amazing person in you; believe it, take the steps where you value yourself and say there is more out there.

I am so extremely thankful for these experiences even though it was traumatic and took a huge toll on my finances, health, and mental well-being. It has now meant that I am doing my purpose and coming into myself as an artist, poet, and writer. Growing, expanding myself to what my soul was born to do. The gift out of my experience is to be all of me, own my darkness and light, as that makes me a whole person. To be the person that God created me to be.

Also, to fulfil my purpose as to what I am meant to do; that is, to shine a light on bullying, narcissistic behaviour, toxic behaviour in workplaces and our personal lives. Although my experiences were pretty brutal, I am not going to wish this experience away as it has taught me so much and enabled me to become who I am meant to be. We are all where we are meant to be in life. No one is too old or too young to do things. I feel so much more alive coming out of this experience and healing my wounds. I am not going to allow my past to define me and tell me who I should be.

I am no longer in the workforce and instead, I am following the entrepreneurial journey. I decided I wanted to have joy, health, success in my life. Some of the things I enjoyed while working was helping others, educating others, encouraging others, and supporting them, and these are the skills I am taking into the next step in my journey. Nothing I ever did has been wasted, it will all be used for my purpose.

I know I have the choice to be the creator of my own life by removing the old pattern of thinking around my life and creating new ones. You can make that choice and choose a life of joy and meaning.

One day you will tell your story of how you've overcome what you're going through now, and it will become part of someone else's survival guide—Brené Brown.

Hiding in the Shadows

I have been hiding in the shadows
Believing I was not good enough
Or what I had to say was nothing important
When the light came I hid
Downplaying myself
The light kept on knocking at my door
At first softly and then louder and louder
I began to let go of the fear
The more I surrendered
I more I started to spend time in the light
I needed to tell the truth of what happened to me
Without fear or expectations
To step into my true self
To share a story that is healing for me and others
For a purpose that was bigger than me
And the light has shown me the way

Elizabeth Gray 2020

Chapter 1

Choosing Myself

Owning all of me

Having been a victim of multiple bullying attacks, I have asked myself why. Why me? What did I do wrong? What is wrong with me? What could I have done to prevent this? The kind of attacks I have received include intimidation, demanding information, physically standing over me, gaslighting, being watched, humiliation, having other teams members turn against me, being isolated by the team, having lies told about me, having a manager enforce someone else's lies against me, discriminatory comments, comments putting down my work ability, being yelled at to teach me a lesson, people making sure I know that they are superior to me, using information about me against me. I certainly did not ask for this to happen. I had to wonder and look at the journey I had been on in my work and personal life. What was life trying to teach me?

For a long time, I did not understand why the bullying was happening. I believed it was my role to give and give to others and place myself last. This did radiate a message to others that I could be used and abused. I came to accept that this abuse was normal, and I could not expect anything different in my life. I find this very sad, writing the previous sentence that abuse was normal to me.

As a young child, I was not taught to value or love myself. The messages I heard through my life were that there was something wrong with me, that I was the problem, what use was I, everything was my fault. I felt that I was not good enough to receive good things in my life. Often my voice was devaluated and if I talked, I was dismissed, and it was implied that my own role was to support people to help them achieve. Nowhere was it mentioned what I could achieve in my life or how they could support me. It was definitely a one-way street. So, I cast myself into a support role, cheering on, encouraging other people, helping them out for the nil or meagre tokens of appreciation.

I am so grateful for the friends that valued and loved me as without them I would not have survived the bullying. Their support through the difficult times was amazing and I loved the fact that my friends were so angry on my behalf; it took me a while to be angry for myself. I should have been so angry earlier, and I was not as the abuse was normal to me and I did not expect anything different. Also, the fear generated by the bullies played a part in me not speaking up.

There is a norm of being silent around bullying and toxic behaviour. I did not deserve the bullying and abuse and it is the other person's behaviour and often it comes from their ego and insecurity. Those with toxic behaviour are attached to ensuring they maintain their status quo at all costs, which is mainly at the cost of the victim. Also, there is a lot of shaming of the victim that it was their fault, and they are responsible for it; this often triggers our childhood shame. **NO, we did not ask for the abuse,** as the behaviour says more about the abusers.

As a result of my experience, I found people with bullying behaviour have the need to be in control to feel safe, feel superior over others, want all the attention and recognition. I found a lot of these people had very dominant personalities and were in your face demanding their needs from you and having no respect for your boundaries. I have had health challenges my whole life and when you are not well it is difficult to think clearly and have the energy to interact with these types of people.

Dealing with bullying behaviour

How do you deal with the bullying behaviour? I am highly sensitive and an empath and found that other people's energies had an impact on my energy. Quite often I found myself being mocked as I was upset by things people said and did. The comments from the bullies told me that what I thought and felt was of no importance and did not matter and only their view of the situation was the correct one.

The agenda with bullying is to get you to see things in the way they see things and to get you to do what they want you to do. They often twist the facts, make judgements about you, and want you to feel that there is something wrong with you. Often, they will suggest that you develop a harder skin and that feeling emotions is wrong.

There was not a lot of information around dealing with other people's energies when I was growing up. I did not gain a lot of knowledge around this until recently. Often being an empath is mocked and considered as woo woo. But being an empath is part of who I am. I can walk into a room and tell if energy is high or low. I can also pick up when someone is sad or has an issue that they want to talk about. I can pick up on who a person is and whether I will have problems with them. I am in the process of learning how to be an empowered empath that is able to deal with other people's energies in a healthy way.

The main thing I have learned from these toxic experiences is to value myself and choose myself over other people. I matter and what I do with my life matters. Within my soul which I am so grateful for is a sense of self-preservation that has come into force to enable me to leave these types of relationships. The choice I had in staying would have been to leave me broken as a person, controlled and knowing they believed that they had the right to walk over me, threaten me, and keep me in fear of them. Often the choice has been between leaving and healing or having an income. I have had blessings with some funds to help me through this process. But I should not have had to do that. I have also decided that this way of being had to stop. I wanted more in my life than being abused. **I want to matter.** Why put myself back into being in someone else's process that does not bring out the best in me?

Another part of the puzzle that I have learnt is that I needed to put boundaries around the toxic behaviour. In the past I have found when I have put boundaries in there is a fight back from the person who liked that there were no boundaries before. The challenges to manage other people's behaviours will continue to come up, as that is life. I am getting better at this as I practise more and find ways to deal with unacceptable behaviour.

The workplace is a lot harder to manage as there are complaint systems, hierarchy, power, ego, working-hard attitude, management systems, employee review systems, favouritism, maintenance of the status quo, intimidation, do it, don't complain, misuse of power, and being tough. Some workplaces run on the masculine side of living, which is all about doing, being strong, showing no signs of weakness, sucking it up, managing it, controlling it, and working long hours. For many years, I did the masculine thing—working hard and putting all of me into a workplace, expecting rewards for the work I did but ultimately on many occasions found myself been used.

I ended up being disconnected from myself and having separate feminine and masculine sides. I realised I put too much energy into the workplace as this is where I thought the rewards would come from. I was not balanced in the many areas of my life. My health suffered as I continued to do the masculine way in the workplace. When I look back at my life, the healthier workplaces had a balanced way and looked after the employees. These places appreciated me and what I had to offer, and it was mutual, not a one-way street. The lessons for me from toxic behaviour in the workplace was to change my life and not keep a ladder up a wall that was not supporting me and was in fact damaging to me.

I also made the decision that I was not going to put myself in the same situation again. The damage to my health and mindset was huge and the implications are still being felt today in my life. I decided that I wanted to work for myself and do more of what I loved. I had heard the message so many times about doing what you love but I could not believe it would be true for me. As part of my healing process, I started to do more of the things I loved—writing poetry, painting, and doing art. I loved when I did art school—the freedom and creativity of experimenting and having fun was fantastic. I did so much of my creativity there.

Unfortunately, I had the belief that artists or creative people don't make money and I sold myself out to the corporate world for income and things. It seemed if you did not have a job that you were not worthy. Having joy in your life is so important, it keeps everything running. I did not want to get to retirement age and then live retired. There is so much more in me to give and grow in the world. There are so many possibilities out there.

Choosing the life of an entrepreneur is so different and challenging to someone that always had a job and thought that was the only way to earn income. The change of the mindset of employee to entrepreneur has been shaky and full of doubts, fear, and courage. It was such a twist that I needed to conquer and to even give myself permission to do it and learn that it was achievable for me. I am so new on this journey and still struggle with finding courage to put myself out there and have a voice. A voice that I denied to myself for so long. I don't want to be silent anymore. Silent is being compliant and no more; I want to be myself and live my life differently from what other people expect me to do.

Why choosing yourself is important and not selfish

> *Do what you feel in your heart to be right—for you'll be criticized anyway. You'll be damned if you do, and damned if you don't—*
> **Eleanor Roosevelt.**

The most important thing you can do is choose yourself as you won't make everyone happy. **You do matter, as does your purpose.** I felt I was trained to put everyone before me and that my job was to keep them happy. When we keep putting other people before ourselves, we are not happy or don't have joy as we can never, never please other people. Choosing ourselves is not selfish and we are choosing ourselves to be fulfilled and thriving and being filled up before we can serve others. We all know the drill on the aeroplane where in an emergency you put on your own mask first before helping others. We need to do this in our lives, put on our own mask first by looking after our bodies and minds so we can operate from fullness rather than emptiness. I know what it is like to operate from empty—it leads to burnout.

At one stage, I worked a full-time job, a part-time job, and was studying part time at university. I had one day off in 14 days. I was leaving home at 7:00 a.m. Monday to Friday to go to university before work and on Monday to Thursday nights after work I went to university and then got home around

10:00 p.m. Not a healthy way to live. This is often taught, that you have to work very hard and be busy and this makes you a success. When you give and give, and other people take, it is not good. The healthy, balanced individuals will give and take while the unhealthy ones take and take.

You are not broken

Too often we are told that we are broken, that there is something wrong with us, that we need to be fixed. One of the best things one of my coaches told me was that I was not broken. This stopped the constant need for me to keep finding what was wrong with me and to fix myself. In reality, I was running unhealthy habits and beliefs in myself from unhealed wounds. What I needed was to believe in myself and see my worth and stop the unhealthy/unresourceful things I was doing. The behaviour I had was not serving me to achieve my highest purpose.

> *Don't devalue ourselves because someone else can't see our self-worth*—**Anonymous**.

Too often with bullying, especially gaslighting, the message coming to us is that we don't know what we are doing or think that what we do is not good enough. The messages deflect from them onto us as being the problem. Gaslighting does so much damage to our sense of ourselves as we are being mentally undermined. We should not allow ourselves to be defined by someone else as to what they think we should do and who we should be. Sometimes people like parents and teachers who are trying to be helpful don't always understand that we have our own message and role inside of us. We need to get to know ourselves, what we truly want and need and what our role is to serve in the world. We can begin by helping one person at a time.

It is always easier to look at someone else and see all of their strengths and weaknesses and think you know what they should be doing. People have their own journey to go on and may not be ready to see what you see. Encourage people first.

The inner work is painful but also very liberating, facing our dark side and the bits we don't like about ourselves. Doing the inner work is a continual journey of changing how we think about ourselves. If you look at successful people, the majority have done their inner work. The inner work is about recognising the emotions underlying your feelings (like anger, fear, and sadness) and dealing with them. Also, we need to understand the beliefs that are in our subconscious which are running our operating systems. We can change our thoughts and beliefs.

It is okay to be you, and you matter

All of us matter as we all have something to bring to the world. We all want to be seen, heard, and acknowledged. Too often with bullying and gaslighting we don't receive these things from the other person. Oprah Winfrey[1] says most common desires people have is to be validated and she has summed it up in the following three questions people want after a conversation:

- Did you see me?
- Did you hear me?
- Did what I say mean anything to you?

We all have been created for a purpose and all are required in the world. We should not let other people tell us otherwise. Cathy Heller says, "God does not create extras."

---

[1] Oprah Winfrey, The Oprah Winfrey Show Finale, oprah.com https://www.oprah.com/oprahshow/the-oprah-winfrey-show-finale_1/7, page 7

There is a specific purpose we have here on earth. Listening to our hearts is so important as God has implanted our purpose in our heart and soul. We need to look after our inner child and souls. Nurture them, like we would a plant, feed and water them. Our soul is so precious. We are not rubbish or anything else. Too often we don't protect ourselves from other people's hurts and ideas. We need to develop a way to sieve out the unwanted or unhelpful stuff. We need boundaries.

We need to try and put ourselves in other people's shoes and listen. Sometimes we don't understand what the person is saying or thinking and in these cases the best we can do is acknowledge that they feel this way, and this is their point of view. So much goodwill can be obtained this way. If you keep on pushing your own agenda in conversations this is not good. Too often in a conversation we are thinking of the next thing to say instead of really listening. To really listen to another person is a wonderful gift. We all want to be listened to, but we won't be listened to unless we listen to others. In a relationship, one of the most damaging things is to wipe off and reject another human being's feelings. None of us is perfect and we all will make mistakes, but we need to be mindful of how we treat others. We need to treat each other as we treat ourselves.

We all want to know that our lives are meant for something and that we matter. We often spend a lot of time looking for our purpose. The fact we are here on earth and have a purpose means we matter. Even if our life is only helping one person, we matter. Don't let anyone else convince you otherwise. Listen to Beyoncé's song "I Was Here": these are very powerful words about making an impact.

Having the freedom to be ourselves and loving ourselves is such a wonderful gift. Tapping into our authenticity and being

Elizabeth Gray

us, who we were meant to be. It is so freeing so feel and know that you are home in your body. Time to dig deep inside.

THE GEMS WITHIN

To find the gems within
To fossick and dig
To bring them to the surface
They may look like rocks
And don't seem to be valuable
But you need to work on the rocks
Polish them up
Give them the best cut to show the light
Of whom you are

Elizabeth Gray 2020

Chapter 2

Societal Expectations

What is expected of us?

Social norms are unwritten rules that govern how people are expected to act in certain situations. This may differ from group to group. This means your behaviour and duties are expected to fit into these rules. Depending on where you are born, your sex, political structure, culture, and religious practice will determine often what the social norms are. Often these social norms are quite fixed and there is shame applied if you want or do anything different. If you want to put yourself first, others may call you selfish, but looking after yourself is not selfish.

When I was growing up, the social expectations for me were go to school, do Year 12, and then go on to university and get a job. Then you get married, have kids, buy a house, work until you retire, and then get to do things you love. Another is the expectations of women that they give and give and make themselves small and taking care of themselves is viewed as selfish. Women are expected to sacrifice themselves for others. These examples are a few and there are plenty of other society/cultural expectations in our lives. What are the ones ruling your life?

Societal expectations are quite often reinforced on TV, social media, religion, and by those in power. There are a lot of marketing messages of how you should be, what you should weigh, how you should look. I don't know if you remember a while ago having a gap through your two front teeth was unacceptable and then all of a sudden Georgia May Jagger had a gap between her front teeth. Now it is fashionable to have the gap between the teeth. Different fads and fashions come and go. When are we ever going to get the message that it's okay to be authentic, unique and yourself? We are all okay, we are not broken or don't need to change ourselves to suit others.

In more recent years, we have been taught to focus on external things to fill us up. For example, success is often defined as having the perfect partner or marriage, expensive car and clothes, a designer watch, the biggest house on the street. A lot of messages have been how the body should look, i.e., being thin, having a tan, whether you should have body hair in particular places, large boobs or butt. Other messages are focused on brands, like having a handbag from certain brands, i.e., where your jeans and shoes should come from. We are told by advertisers, etc. that these things will make us happy, but external things don't make you happy—**only you** can make yourself happy and have joy.

It is time that we define what success means for us. Having a roof over our head, food and clothing, partner, good friends, freedom, being fulfilled, doing the work you love. Think about what success means for you.

Another norm for me was that you had to be polite at all times and you did not say rude things to others. You certainly did not go and upset others. I was taught that I was responsible for any interaction with other people and if they were upset with me that it was my fault. These deeply factored into my life as I took on the responsibility for their reactions. People have triggers and they are responsible for how they react to me. I have been the target of people not taking responsibility for their responses too many times. I have had to learn what my triggers are and how I respond as well. There is a tiny gap between when you are triggered, and this is the time you choose to react or respond.

Society keeps us silent on certain issues such as domestic violence, child abuse, rape, sexual harassment, bullying, narcissist abuse, and gaslighting. Shaming is one of the lowest vibrations and is used often to put people in their place. They make any victim ashamed of what happened to them even if it is not their fault. They blame them that they did not stop it happening or make out they are weak because they allowed it to happen. **NOBODY CHOOSES THESE THINGS TO HAPPEN TO THEM.** The person who took the action to act on this type of behaviour is responsible for it.

Being defined

Too often we allow ourselves to be defined by other people. We contort ourselves into what their view of us is. We hear constant messages that we should be like this, feel like this, act like this. We did not feel that we were enough unless we had people approve of us. No-one should be made to become someone that they are not. People have to respect who a person is and not try and put their stamp on them or expect them to be anything but what they are.

The definitions society puts on us are what a good wife or good mother looks like. What an employee should be doing, i.e., available all the time, putting their work first, staying back without notice, obeying their managers, being a yes person, accepting the rules laid down to them.

As human beings we have to expect more of others in how they treat us and if they don't treat us better we need to put up boundaries and let them know that their behaviour is unacceptable. Sometimes this is very difficult, and we are fearful of their reactions and too often conversations go unsaid.

Other people's messages

Often people are well meaning when they offer you advice. They can be a great sounding board. Sometimes, however, this can be from their point of view of what they would or would not do. They might see what you are doing and find it quite fearful for them to do that or they think it is a crazy idea, so they dissuade you from following the messages you get. We often give more credence to our people's advice than our own soul trying to tell us a message. We also look to receiving confirmation from others that we are on the right track but sometimes we have to keep our dreams to ourselves or only tell individuals that we know will encourage our dreams and support us.

I don't know whether you've heard of the saying that you shouldn't accept criticism from someone you wouldn't ask for advice from. I think we need to keep that in mind if someone gives us some feedback or advice: is this someone we trust that the advice/criticism is constructive? If not, examine whether it is valid and if it is not, ignore it.

The constant criticism from others of how I should be continued for far too long because I was a people pleaser. I found myself contorting to what they wanted me to do but this was not congruent with what was inside me and my authentic self. I needed to do what was right for me and it was very hard with other people telling me what I should think and feel, and how I should act. However, over time, I learnt to listen to my voice. My voice is very important as it expresses what is in my heart and soul.

Life is too short to follow someone else's dreams and I've done that my whole life. I've been the good girl; I've done the right thing that was expected of me, going to work for a living. I continued this even when I was screaming in my soul that it wasn't right for me. We too often allow their opinions to determine what we do in our lives.

Playing small

Often, we are rewarded for playing small in our lives as we don't show up with our mission. We often downplay our worth and what we can do. Playing small does not allow our messages or our purpose to get out there. Often others want us to play small so they can shine. We are meant to shine and bring our skills to the world. Marianne Williamson's quote below is about our fears about playing small and how this does not serve the world.

> *Our deepest fear is not that we are inadequate. Our deepest fear is that we are powerful beyond measure. It is our light, not our darkness that most frightens us. We ask ourselves, who am I to be brilliant, gorgeous, talented, fabulous? Actually, who are you not to be? You are a child of God. You're playing small does not serve the world. There is nothing enlightened about shrinking so that other people won't feel insecure around you. We are all meant to shine, as children do. We were born to make manifest the glory of God that is within us. It is not just in some of us; it is in everyone. And as we let our own light shine, we unconsciously give other people permission to do the same. As we are liberated from our own fear, our presence automatically liberates others.*

Staying safe

Too often we are taught to take the safe route and not take any risks. What I learned was to take the safe route, i.e., get a job, work for a living, don't risk investing on the stock exchange, don't take risks. Also, society is about being safe: get a job, rely on an employer to pay you, save money, buy a house, etc. Through the school system, we are taught to get a job. Even the political rhetoric is about getting a job. However, when you look around there are entrepreneurs or small business owners but some of these still have a job and not a business as they are trading time for money. Often people that take risks go all in and put what they have on where they want to be. There can be no gain without some risk. Playing safe means playing small and stuck.

Following someone else' ideas for your life won't bring you happiness or success. To find these you must follow your own path—Elizabeth Gray.

Deep Wounds

Some wounds are so deep
As is the pain
The default is to bury, deny or mask it
This causes it only to go deeper
And create even more pain
Healing can only come with acknowledging
Sitting with the pain and feeling
No matter how hard or raw
The pain must be felt
Crying can release it
As does pray
As is writing the pain out
The healing with come slowly
And the days will become better
The silver lining will appear
And the blessings can be seen
As is the gift that was within the pain
The growth and mission to serve
To leave a legacy to help others with the pain
Turning everything into circle

Elizabeth Gray 2020

Chapter 3

Highly Sensitive Person and Empaths

For many years, I did not understand that I was an empath and was highly sensitive. I felt other people's emotions and could quickly spot when a person was down or there was something wrong. For me, when I walked into a room I could tell if the energy was up or down. I remember going for a job interview and one of the people in the interview had such low energy that I found it difficult to maintain high energy during the interview. I feel energy deeply and I have struggled with how to deal with other people's energy and become easily overwhelmed. Spending a long time in noisy, crowded environments becomes draining and I need time alone to recover. Empaths like me often care too much and feel with the person suffering. Due to being highly sensitive, I often find it difficult to deal with criticism that may bounce off another person.

Highly sensitive person

"A highly sensitive person (HSP) experiences the world differently than others. Due to a biological difference that they're born with, highly sensitive people are more aware of subtleties and process information deeply. This means they tend to be creative, insightful, and empathetic, but it also means they're more prone than others to stress and overwhelm.

Although being highly sensitive is completely normal — meaning, it's not a disease or a disorder — it's often misunderstood, because only 15 to 20 percent of the population are HSPs"[2]

Being highly sensitive means I feel things deeply. Often highly sensitive people are regarded as being weak for having these traits and this can be viewed as a personality flaw. However,

---

[2] Jenn Granneman "21 Signs You're a Highly Sensitive Person", Highly Sensitive Refuge, published December 13, 2019, https://highlysensitiverefuge.com/highly-sensitive-person-signs/

highly sensitivity is a superpower. Highly sensitive people can be the best performers in an office due to their high EQ (emotional intelligence), have a high level of self-awareness, are detail-oriented, have creativity, and make great leaders. For those who are highly sensitive, this means they are aware of other people's emotions and needs and the energy they are showing. Often, there is a gut feel if there is something wrong in the other person's behaviour.

Empath

A definition of an empath in Merriam-Webster Dictionary[3] is "one who experiences emotions of others." Most empaths are highly sensitive but not all people who are highly sensitive are empaths.

An empath is someone who is highly aware of the emotions of those around them, to the point of feeling those emotions themselves. Empaths see the world differently than other people; they're keenly aware of others, their pain points, and what they need emotionally.

But it's not just emotions. According to Dr. Judith Orloff, author of *The Empath's Survival Guide*[4], empaths can feel physical pain, too—and can often sense someone's intentions or where they're coming from. Andre Soló, says "empaths seem to pick up on many of the lived experience of those around them."[5]

---

[3] Merriam-webster.com, https://www.merriam-webster.com/dictionary/empath

[4] Orloff, Judith, The Empath's Survival Guide – Life Strategies for Sensitive People, London, St Martins Press, 2019

[5] Andre Soló, "13 Signs That You're an Empath", Highly Sensitive Refuge, January 18, 2019. https://highlysensitiverefuge.com/empath-signs/

Being an empath is often called woo woo by people, but it exists. We have all been trained not to take notice of our feelings and intuition. Empaths can feel energy at different levels, and many have insight into what other people feel. It is important to understand that energy from other people can be absorbed, one way to deal with this, it is to send it back to them with love. This is a way of having boundaries and removing yourself from some situations is necessary for your health. Being an empath is a wonderful gift and you need to own it. It can also give you insight into other people. I used to allow other people to put me down for being sensitive and perceptive. Now I acknowledge and appreciate being an empath. But I also had to make choices to be an empowered empath.

When I was growing up, there was not much information around about being an empath or being highly sensitive. I never knew what these traits were called or how to deal with them. I have in the past struggled to find a way to acknowledge this incredible gift and manage other people's energy. If you are wondering about feeling energy, I think most people will understand as we go through COVID-19 that there is a lot of shaming, guilt, and anger going around. We can feel that there is a heaviness in the world as people are struggling with all the restrictions and fear around COVID-19. Most people will have had difficulty dealing with COVID-19 in one way or another due to the pandemic being a massive change in our lives. This type of energy I pick up and feel intensely.

I am learning and finding ways to deal with other people's energies. For too long, feeling these energies made me feel drained, especially the bad behaviour from other people. I went to yoga and meditation, and this has helped me relax. I also have done Brain Heart Coherence meditation to help lift my energy up to the vibration of love which is one of the highest levels. Shame, guilt and anger are at the lower levels of vibration.

I am also an introvert and, according to Dr. Elaine Aron[6], 70% of highly sensitive people are introverts. Introverts prefer small groups over large groups and don't like crowds and noise and need lots of quiet time to recover and enjoy quieter activities like reading. 'Being an introvert is genetic, and it involves differences in how the brain processes dopamine, the "reward" chemical.'[7]

I often find it hard to express what I think and feel due to my high sensitivity, and people often dismiss what I think and feel. Often people don't understand what an empath may be deeply feeling.

There are a number of things empaths can do to help deal with other people's energies and these include:

- Remove yourself from toxic people
- Take walks in nature
- Say no
- Imagine a boundary of light around yourself
- Detox from media and others
- Have long baths

---

[6] Andre Soló, The Difference Between Introverts, Empaths, and Highly Sensitive People, Highly Sensitive Refuge, June 17, 2020, https://highlysensitiverefuge.com/empaths-highly-sensitive-people-introverts/

[7] Andre Soló, The Difference Between Introverts, Empaths, and Highly Sensitive People, Highly Sensitive Refuge, June 17, 2020, https://highlysensitiverefuge.com/empaths-highly-sensitive-people-introverts/

Paranoia

Our brains have a basis towards a negative bias and we often look to confirm when bad things happen that everything that is happening to us is bad. One day while working, I saw an email that was sent around about myself between some colleagues in the department. It was noticeable that the person with the bullying behaviour was dividing the department up with the majority on that person's side. Having other people in the department being targeted as well helped me deal with it because it was not all about me. Another colleague resigned due to this person's behaviour. Due to the stress of this job, some of my hair fell out for a period of time and never grew back completely.

As a result of the numerous episodes in this workplace, I started to interpret everything that was happening in the office as a personal attack on me. In the end, I had to decide that unless the bullying is obvious, I will accept that everything is normal. This stopped me from having paranoia and enabled me to view some of the events with more perspective. Doing this made a difference for me psychologically. I am grateful for the pause, and this allowed me space to understand what was going on.

Intuition and red flags

Cambridge Dictionary defines intuition as "knowledge from an ability to understand or know something immediately based on your feelings rather than facts."[8]

For me, my intuition comes from my heart and gives me whispers around what I should be doing. We can often dismiss

---

[8] Cambridge Dictionary, dictionary.cambridge.com, https://dictionary.cambridge.org/dictionary/english/intuition

our intuition, but it will keep on giving us messages until we take notice. Sometimes feelings can be misleading but other times they can be spot on.

A red flag 'is something that gives a warning of trouble'.[9] People through their behaviour give us clues all the time. With both intuition and red flags, we often override them with our logical brain and think things will be okay instead of trusting ourselves. Having intuition and knowing the red flags at work and in your life can be very important, especially if you take note of the messages people do tell you and they do tell you a lot about themselves. Sometimes there is an off feeling, or you know that there is going to be a problem. I have found this to be useful in picking up signs in workplaces and job interviews. We need to take note of the messages that we are receiving.

I found one job interview quite disturbing as when the interviewer first saw me, they deliberately looked me up and down my body and I felt very uneasy. Then in the interview, they went through my resume and made disparaging comments about my skills. Fortunately for me I did not get the job. I ended up reporting the person's behaviour to the employment agency.

Sometimes you get a sinking feeling from meeting someone. At another meeting I attended the person said something in a way that made it quite apparent of their own importance and knowledge. I instantly knew that this person was probably going to create problems for me and there were quite a few issues with this person.

---

[9] Your Dictionary, yourdictionary.com, https://www.yourdictionary.com/red-flag

Another time, there was a very slight clue that I dismissed at the time. This involved two people from the particular workplace interviewing me. At the end, one of them got up and flicked their head in a strange way. Ultimately, when I look back, as I got the job, it was definitely a clue to that person's behaviour and what was in store for me.

So please, take note when you go for job interviews: no job or income is worth your value, worth, or income. Ask questions regarding management styles and watch for visual clues they give out and how they treat you.

Forgive yourself for not knowing what you didn't know before you learned it
—Maya Angelou.

Listen to the Heart

Listen to the heart
Listen to the dreams
Allow the dreams to be planted
Give the seeds the sun and rain
Some will die and some will live
We will learn and it is okay to fail
That is part of our journey
The challenges and obstacles will rise
Focus on the solutions and the way forward
Keep on going if you stumble
Continue to take action
Be at peace and enjoy the journey
It is never about the destination
It is about how you grow and who you will become

Elizabeth Gray 2020

Part Two
Bullying

People who are hurting inside lash out and hurt other people. The more we love ourselves the less damage we do—Elizabeth Gray

Gaslighting

The drip feed of negativity was easily missed
But the results were not
I found that I was doubting and second guessing myself
My radiance and lightness was no more
My smile faded as did my health
Now I see
I wondered how could I have prevented this
I had stopped looking for the positive
and focused on the negative
But when I look inside I still have me
One who can again smile and be radiant
One who can soar high in the sky
One who can be content knowing that they are enough
One who knows that everything will be right in the end

Elizabeth Gray 2020

Chapter 4

Bullying, Narcissistic, and Gaslighting Behaviour

Some people try to be tall by cutting off the heads of others—Paramahansa Yogananda.

My aim of this chapter is to help people see the signs of bullying, narcissistic, abusive, and gaslighting behaviour.

Bullying behaviour

Headsup.org.au states "Workplace bullying is **repeated** and **unreasonable** behaviour directed towards an employee or group of employees, that creates **a risk to health and safety.**"[10]

"Bullying is usually seen as acts or verbal comments that could 'mentally' hurt or isolate a person in the workplace. Sometimes, bullying can involve negative physical contact as well. Bullying usually involves repeated incidents or a pattern of behaviour that is intended to intimidate, offend, degrade or humiliate a particular person or group of people. It has also been described as the assertion of power through aggression"[11]

Examples of bullying behaviour are:

- Intimidation
- Mind games
- Teasing and playing practical jokes
- Shouting
- Unwanted physical contact
- Treating someone differently from how others are treated
- Negative comments
- Belittling what a person says

---

[10] Workplace Bullying, Headsup.org, https://www.headsup.org.au/healthy-workplaces/workplace-bullying

[11] Bullying in the Workplace, ccohs.ca, https://www.ccohs.ca/oshanswers/psychosocial/bullying.html

- Spying on or stalking a person
- Changing someone's work responsibilities without cause
- Socially isolating or excluding someone
- Giving incorrect information or withholding information
- Spreading rumours or gossip
- Criticising person constantly
- Making difficult deadlines for an employee to achieve

Bullying can happen from manager to employee, employee to employee, and employee to manager. It does not discriminate between levels. It can also exist within families, romantic relationships, and other types of relationships.

Narcissistic behaviour

Helpguide.org states "**Narcissistic personality disorder** involves a pattern of self-centered, arrogant thinking and **behaviour**, a lack of empathy and consideration for other people, and an excessive need for admiration. Others often describe people with NPD as cocky, manipulative, selfish, patronizing, and demanding."[12]

There is an attraction/link between empaths and narcissistic behaviour. As empaths we need to stop attracting narcissistic behaviour into our lives; this is because we give and give and the narcissistic behaviour is about taking.

Narcissistic behaviour is when a person needs attention and recognition in their lives. They also like to have control of others and often conversations are one way from them to

---

[12] Narcissistic Personality Disorder, helpguide.org, https://www.helpguide.org/articles/mental-disorders/narcissistic-personality-disorder.htm

you. They are unaware of everyone else's needs. People with narcissistic behaviour are manipulative and place the blame and guilt on other people. Usually this is an empath.

Sometimes, the person with the narcissistic behaviour enrols other people in attacking their victim. These people are known as flying monkeys. The term flying monkeys came from the film *The Wizard of Oz* where the Wicked Witch sent the flying monkeys to get Dorothy and her dog. In one workplace, I had the person with the narcissistic behaviour turn a number of my colleagues against me and I remember one of these making a few nasty comments to me. The narcissists also want other people to turn against you so the truth about them is not revealed.

Sometimes, other people when they know that the person with the narcissistic behaviour does not like a particular person, they can use this situation to their advantage by manipulating the narcissistic to get what they want.

Narcissistic supply

"Narcissistic supply is a form of psychological addiction and dependency, where the narcissist requires (demands) constant importance, 'special treatment,' validation, and/or appeasement in order to feel good about him or herself. This insatiable craving to be 'put on a pedestal' explains to a large extent the narcissist's sense of conceit, entitlement, and self-absorption".[13]

Narcissistic people constantly need a supply of attention and they position themselves as superior or are a controller or like

---

[13] Ni, Preston. "7 Ways Narcissists Manipulate Relationships", psychologytoday.com, https://www.psychologytoday.com/au/blog/communication-success/201903/7-ways-narcissists-manipulate-relationships

breaking boundaries. A victim provides the narcissistic supply whether it be positive or negative supply.

Positive supply is where you give them attention, admiration and make yourself subservient to them. Whereas "negative supply is typically the product of any action taken to trigger you. Specifically, your emotional reaction".[14]

Some examples of narcissistic supply are:

- Wanting special treatment
- Feeling they have control over you
- Knowing that you dislike or fear them
- Having attention
- Being praised
- Be winning
- They suck the energy out of you
- Knowing they can affect your mind

False self

The person with NPD (Narcissistic Personality Disorder) also has a false self that they have to maintain. The false self is what they believe about themselves, i.e., they are superior and smarter than everyone else and when this is threatened, they will do anything to defend it. And if it means destroying people, they will do it.

"This false self is also sometimes seen as the "idealised self" or the self through which we operate because our true self just somewhere along the line (usually quite young) felt too weak,

---

[14] Narcwisemaggie, How to starve the narcissist of supply, narcwise.com https://narcwise.com/2018/10/02/starve-narcissist-supply, October 2, 2018

inadequate, or overwhelmed to function and gain approval in the situation in which it found itself."[15]

Sam Vaknin, narcissist and the author of *Malignant Self Love: Narcissism Revisited*, says, the false self has two functions:

- Acts as a decoy and it is tough and can take the pain
- The false self is used by the narcissist as the true self, and they view themselves as deserving better.[16]

Having both of these functions is essential to the narcissist's survival. The narcissist also has the ability to find a person's wounds and target these and manipulate the victim.

Gaslighting behaviour

The term gaslighting came from a movie from 1944 (and prior to that the play Gas Light) where a husband manipulates his wife, so she thinks she is losing touch with reality. The motive by the husband is to have his wife committed to a mental institution in order to steal her inheritance.

"Gaslighting is a form of persistent manipulation and brainwashing that causes the victim to doubt her or himself, and ultimately lose her or his own sense of perception, identity, and self-worth."[17] Gaslighting is done over time so the victim does not realise what has happened.

---

[15] Dayton, Dr Tian, "Creating A False Self: Learning To Live A Lie", huffpost.com, https://www.huffpost.com/entry/creating-a-false-self-lea_b_269096, updated November 17, 2011

[16] Vaknin, Sam, The Dual Role of the False Self, healthyplace.com, https://www.healthyplace.com/personality-disorders/malignant-self-love/dual-role-of-the-false-self

[17] Ni, Preston, 7 Stages of Gaslighting in a Relationship, psychologytoday.com, https://www.psychologytoday.com/au/blog/communication-success/201704/7-stages-gaslighting-in-relationship, April 30, 2017

Gaslighting is done by manipulation and by sowing the seeds of doubt of who they are and their ability. It is emotional abuse. This can be done by undermining the person or minimising them and their concerns. Often the reasons to gaslight someone is to gain control or change a person. Some of the tactics include:

- Trivialising what the victim feels and thinks
- Countering where the abuser offers information that comes from their perspective
- Keeping information from victim
- Diverting and blocking victim's attention
- Verbal abuse
- Undermining the victim/blaming them
- Forgetting/denial of what was previously said
- Reframing information that they are right

To identify when you have experienced gaslighting, these are some of what you may feel:

- You know something is wrong but can't pinpoint it
- Doubt what you think and feel
- Find yourself less confident than you were in the past
- Feel you are too sensitive
- Struggle to make decisions

The person that is gaslighting sees relationships not in a collaborative way but in a competitive way where one person needs to win and that is them. They also create an image of being dominant and want others to submit to them. People who gaslight others are all about dominance and control. They will become angry and hostile when people don't do what they want. They are good at hiding their insecurity.

I was being gaslighted in one of my jobs and I did not realise what was happening. I spoke to someone about how my reality felt over my work as I was not trusting my judgement as I did previously. The person I spoke to suggested that I was being gaslighted. After that it made perfect sense to me. For me the worst part of the gaslighting was the trivialisation and minimisation of what I thought and felt. To have your thoughts and feelings wiped as nothing is horrific; it is like you don't exist. I remember in a meeting when I was discussing what I felt and thought that it was like a ping pong match with the trivialisations coming back over the net, counteracting what I said. Also, the blame and deflection were directed to me as being the issue and that their perspective was correct. It highlighted to me that they did not really want to solve the issues.

"Many narcissists and gaslighters have thin skin and can react poorly when called to account for their negative behavior. When challenged, the narcissist is likely to either fight (e.g. temper tantrum, excuse-making, denial, blame, hypersensitivity) or take flight (bolt out the door, avoidance, silent treatment, sulking resentment, or other forms of passive-aggression). The gaslighter nearly always resorts to escalation by doubling or tripling down on their false accusations or coercions, to intimidate or oppress their opponent. Many gaslighters view relationships as inherently competitive rather than collaborative; a zero-sum game where one is either a winner or a loser, on top or at the bottom. 'Offense is the best defense' is a mantra for many gaslighters, which also represents their aggressive method of relating to people."[18]

---

[18] Ni, Preston, 6 Common Traits of Narcissists and Gaslighters, psychologytoday.com, https://www.psychologytoday.com/au/blog/communication-success/201707/6-common-traits-narcissists-and-gaslighters, July 30, 2017

The main aim of a narcissist's behaviour is that they want to control you. Dr. Les Carter[19] defines what people with bullying behaviour want from you and these are:

- Acknowledge that they are superior to you
- View yourself as they view you (you are less than them)
- Fit into their mould
- Stroke their ego
- Know that your feelings and thoughts are irrelevant
- Accept that you are at fault

These are unreasonable and unhealthy requests and if you think you can have a normal conversation with them, think again. The conversation will be turned around to you being the problem. The more you explain yourself to them, the more this will be used against you. In addition, they don't care about you and your feelings.

What are the characteristics you have that narcissists target?

Narcissists like easy targets and don't waste time on people that are not able to manipulate.

"A common misconception is that narcissists go for the weak, because they are easier to manipulate. In fact, narcissists prefer to try and hook someone in who is strong-willed, and who has talents or characteristics they admire. That way, they feel more accomplished if they succeed in tearing them down."[20]

---

[19] Carter, Dr Les, Surviving Narcissism TV on YouTube
[20] Dodgson, Lindsay. The 4 types of people narcissists are attracted to, according to a psychotherapist, businessinsider.com, https://www.businessinsider.com/the-types-of-people-narcissists-are-attracted-to-2018-8?r=AU&IR=T, August 7, 2018.

The characteristics that a narcissist looks for are:

- No or little boundaries
- Care for other people
- Have empathy
- People pleaser
- Always doing the right thing
- People that are forgiving
- Needing other people's approval
- Being selfless
- Responsible and reliable
- Lacking self-worth
- Have insecurities
- Self-sufficient
- Trusting
- Loyal
- Likes to avoid conflict
- Have unresolved trauma
- Easy going
- Talented
- Successful
- Will accept the behaviour from the narcissists as normal (due patterning from childhood or other relationships with narcissists)
- People that reflect well on them (this is by association)
- People that overlook their flaws

Narcissists are searching for people that make them feel better and complete them. Narcissists also want to take away and destroy the good things that their victim has about their life. They also don't want to see other people happy.

Relationships with empaths

There is an attraction between empaths and narcissistic abuse and bullying. Often empaths have a low sense of self and identity and do not value themselves. Empaths are often highly sensitive. Unfortunately, empaths will attract narcissists as the empaths give of themselves and have little or no boundaries and those who are bullying also have no boundaries and take and take. Narcissists are the opposite of empaths as they have no empathy. Narcissists need a supply, and they need you to feed it. Empaths need to value themselves and become empowered as a whole human being, not giving and giving, and put in their boundaries.

SILENCED

My voice was silenced
It was not allowed to be heard
It was trivialised and made to be insignificant
No one has the right to shut people down
What gives you the authority to be all knowing
A title does not make you more worthy
The way you treat people says more about you than me
What are you so afraid of?
That someone might outshine you
Look inside we all have to do the work
Find our voice and be authentic
And most of all be ourselves
Allow ourselves to show our magnificence
Which were created to be

Elizabeth Gray 2020

Chapter 5

Psychological Safety, Misuse of Power, Toxic Workplaces

Psychological safety

Ann Edmondson states, "Psychological safety is a belief that one will not be punished or humiliated for speaking up with ideas, questions, concerns or mistakes."[21]

For an employee to have psychological safety they have to feel safe to voice things and not be judged. In one of my workplaces, I did not have psychological safety as I found when I spoke up using my knowledge and experience, I was put down and humiliated. I had sought help from people in the company as I was being gaslighted but found that they were constantly telling me that I had to talk to my abuser. I know abuser sounds like a strong word but basically with the manipulation and the gaslighting it is bullying and abuse. I certainly did not feel psychologically safe talking to my abuser.

In addition, my abuser was allowed to have control over the process in the meeting and over me. At no point did they actually care and show me compassion for the issues I brought up. It was all about their process and I did not feel that I was considered as a person at all but someone to control. No one should have control over other people. It is all about working together. What happened to respect for each other?

It is hard when you just don't feel safe in the workplace, and you don't know when the person is going to have the next attack on you. You are in constant fear as they can launch it at any time when they feel threatened or jealous.

---

[21] Edmondson, Ann. What is psychological safety and why is it the key to great teamwork?, impraise.com, https://www.impraise.com/blog/what-is-psychological-safety-and-why-is-it-the-key-to-great-teamwork

In one employment situation, a meeting was arranged with an agenda I felt was designed to humiliate me and treat me like I was five years old. Going to this meeting did not make me feel safe and I believed if I went to the meeting, I would have come out of it broken. Instead, I left the workplace.

Companies have policies that allow employees to bring themselves fully to work and have psychological safety. At one workplace neither was granted to me. Continually I was being told that my thoughts and feelings were trivial, but the company did not own my feelings and thoughts and how I interpreted what was said. If I felt threatened, I felt threatened even if the person did not intend it that way. But it was always about how the other person interpreted it; nowhere was there about how I interpreted it.

Misuse of power

Misuse of power occurs in many relationships and workplaces where there is someone that has more power than you. In a workplace the manager has more power than the subordinate. Part of their role is to assess you and your abilities in your role; however, if they are biased or don't like you it is often hard to go over their head and speak to others to get a fair hearing.

If this person has narcissistic personality disorder tendencies and if you do something that they consider is harmful to them, they will go on the attack and use their power, fear, and intimidation to get you back into line.

Those with narcissistic behaviour also do the following when they feel threatened:

- Play victim
- Lie
- Blame others
- Convince others you are the one at fault
- Intimidate
- Destroy property
- Make false accusations
- Insult you

Often when the person with the narcissist behaviour has power and authority over you, they can misuse their position to have complete control over you. If you decide to make a complaint about their behaviour, they can try and distort things and make you appear that you're emotional and you don't know what you're doing and that you're a problem. They may is to slander you and damage your reputation. Narcissists believe they are justified in their behaviour as they believe you deserve it.

How have you been portrayed in the workplace? Often, you have no control over this and sometimes letting go is the only way. The people who know you, know the truth. There may be some stories told about your behaviour or your work. Being bullied does affect your work performance. Nobody asks how this happened and what the specific details are. The assumption is that the other person with the power is telling the truth and often you will not be listened to and it is assumed that you are the bad person. If you are not able to do your work when did this happen, which part of your work are you not doing? Has it been explained to you and has it been agreed on by both parties? Usually, it is management doing top down and there is no agreement or win/win for both of you. Is your manager affecting your ability to work due to bullying and gaslighting?

These questions around how the situation came into being and having the full details are often missed by HR and other management as the manager is believed over the employee. Often the higher layers of management only see things through the eyes of their immediate subordinate rather than have healthy and regular conversations with the employees below their immediate subordinate and really find out what is happening in the business. Nobody asks the rest of them team what they see and think about whether the manager's behaviour is appropriate. This makes the situation one-sided, and management wins.

Relationships between anybody in the business needs to be win/win relationships where both sides win. There needs to be resolutions in the business and not compromises from the employee or manager. Compromises means that someone has given something up whereas a resolution is a solution where both parties agree and win.

It is not healthy for a business where employees have to obey and do what they are told. The other side of the employees being stuck in a losing relationship is it is not healthy emotionally or physically for the employees. If employees are too scared of their boss, they are not able to speak up when things are wrong. This could lead to fraud and other undesirable activities taking place in business. Usually if bullying and gaslighting is going on, this can spread throughout the business and can cause financial losses and disruption to the business.

This misuse of power can affect your career, your mental status and your physical health. Obtaining the right help within the organisation can become too impossible as employees feel too scared to approach the human resources department or don't trust them to do the right thing. Counselling is offered to the employee but this does not solve the problem as the problem lies within the business and not the employee. Usually in these cases, it is not possible to resolve the issue in a normal manner as the playing field is not level.

You may have a relationship with a person in the business and you think it is a good one so you don't believe that they could be bullying their subordinates. Because you have not seen it does not mean it does not exist.

Victim blaming

Victim blaming is where the victim is blamed for what has happened to them rather than the perpetrator who bears full responsibility. Victim blaming suggests that the victim did something to provoke what happened by the way they spoke or acted.

In bullying, it is often the victim that is blamed, i.e., they did not speak up, they were not strong enough, they should have prevented it, they invited it in, if they had issues with the person then they are taking revenge or making a false complaint, etc. The behaviour of the person doing the bullying and their history is not looked into. The blaming of victims often stops them coming forward and reporting what has happened. Also, if the perpetrator is not held accountable and does not learn that their behaviour was wrong, they will continue acting in this way.

"Another issue that contributes to our tendency to blame the victim is known as the hindsight bias.

- When we look at an event that happened in the past, we have a tendency to believe that we should have been able to see the signs and predict the outcome.

- This hindsight makes it seem like the victims of a crime, accident, or another form of misfortune should have been able to predict and prevent whatever problem might have befallen them."[22]

The types of crimes that receive higher victim blaming are sexual assaults. The victim is blamed for the clothing they wore, whether they were drunk or not, whether they had sex before.

Do we blame a pedestrian walking down the street who is hit by a car that is driven by a drunk driver and say that they attracted the car and walked in front of it? Do we blame someone when their car is stolen and question the type and make of the car? Do we not blame the victim when they are robbed by strangers but perhaps blame them when they are robbed by a friend?[23]

The blaming culture needs to be stopped. Bullying is unwanted and uninvited behaviour and the perpetrator's behaviour needs to be addressed, not the victim. Put yourself in the other person's shoes and find out how you would feel if it happened to you. Not stopping this means more people are damaged by the bullying behaviour and this can have serious effects on their mental and physical health and their financial circumstances.

---

[22] Cherry, Kendra. Why Do People Blame the Victim? Verywellmind.com, https://www.verywellmind.com/why-do-people-blame-the-victim-2795911, Fact checked July 23, 2020

[23] Summarised from What is Victim Blaming, itsonusfortcollins,org, http://itsonusfortcollins.org/wp-content/uploads/2017/02/What-is-Victim-Blaming.pdf

Toxic workplaces

> When a workplace becomes toxic, its poison spreads beyond its walls and into the lives of its workers and their families—Gary Chapman

"A toxic work environment is one wherein dysfunction and drama reign, whether it's the result of a narcissistic boss, vindictive co-workers, absence of order, etcetera. Basically, a hostile work environment 'leaves you feeling like dirt,'" says Robert Sutton, a Stanford University professor who studies organisational behaviour and author of *The A**hole Survival Guide*.[24]

In workplaces, there can be toxic employees or management, and they can be in one department or many departments or through the entire company. When toxicity spreads through the organisation, it is like cancer and will costs the business in financial and reputational terms. Toxicity needs to be eliminated from the top down. Sometimes the toxic workers are the high-performance ones and management doesn't want to lose them and may sacrifice the company for them. With toxicity in a work environment, fraud and other illegal activities can become the norm.

On one occasion the manager would not listen to the team who did not want to do a task they felt uncomfortable with. The team felt that what was being asked of them to do was to commit fraud. The manager did not care or listen to the team's concerns instead ordered them to do what they were told. The team then went to another manager and the task was done correctly and fraud was not committed. However, when their

---

[24] Bortz, Daniel. The hostile work environment checklist: How toxic is yours?, monster.com https://www.monster.com/career-advice/article/workplace-checklist-how-toxic-is-yours-hot-jobs

manager was told this, they said to the team, "Why did you not do what you were told?"

Some of the symptoms for toxicity include:

- High level of sick leave
- Narcissistic managers
- High turnover
- Discrimination and harassment
- Management that doesn't listen
- Office politics
- Disrespect for employee's work/life balance
- Negative or poor communication
- Underperformers' behaviour is not addressed
- Gossip and rumours
- Secrecy
- People don't feel free to talk up at meetings
- Everything is focused on measures and not meanings, i.e., what it means to the employees
- Input is not asked for
- Feedback to management is discouraged

A number of ways to prevent or reduce toxicity is:

- Have an anonymous telephone line for employees to report bad behaviour to
- Have an anonymous employee feedback that the employees trust
- Have senior management embody the values of the company i.e., no bullying
- Have an education program for managers to understand bullying and demonstrate bad behaviours

- Have review of managers by their subordinates
- Have normalised behaviour of no toxicity so it is reported and dealt with quickly
- Listen to the employees if they have concerns

Bullying behaviours cost employers in high sick leave, high staff turnover and associated costs, staff doing their jobs without care, increased legal costs and even reputational damage.

Being in the Light

Being in the light
Feels so uncomfortable
It is all so new
I need to stretch more
Helping others with my voice
Telling my story of shame and toxicity
Willing to call others out on their bad behaviour
No longer accepting the blame
For things I have not done or for being myself
I have to be willing to stay in the light
Being no longer fearful of others' actions
To serve those who are afraid of the light
And help them find their light
So the truth can set all of us free

Elizabeth Gray 2020

*You get to decide what
you believe about yourself*
—Martha Beck.

Chapter 6

Being Bullied

> *Don't let someone who did you wrong make you think there's something wrong with you. Don't devalue yourself because they didn't value you. Know your worth even if they don't*—Trent Shelton.

In this chapter and the following one, I am writing how I felt being bullied and the effect of the bullying on myself. I have written this so people can understand what it feels like to be bullied and the impact it has made. By writing these words, it may help others going through work situations and are able to recognise what bullying is. This is also to educate those who have not been bullied to understand the impact of bullying on people. This is not meant to be a poor-me section or a story that I want to keep repeating in the future.

No one asks to be bullied and it is certainly not your fault you were bullied. I repeat, this is not your fault. This behaviour comes from the other person, and you were victim of this type of behaviour. Often the blame is being placed on the victim as if it was your fault that they bullied you. The other person has reasons for their behaviour, but it is not up to you to change their behaviour. However, it is your responsibility for putting boundaries in and for your healing. Fixing the other person is not going to fix you. Forgiving, having gratitude, detaching, and surrendering from these situations takes time.

For me, how do I describe the experience at being at the end of abuse in the form of bullying, narcissism, and gaslighting?

These experiences of abuse have been traumatic, and the attacks were so personal to my identity as a person. Often these attacks come out of jealousy of who you are. I don't know if you realise, but we all show a lot of light. We are not good at recognising our light and all the beautiful things around us.

Elizabeth Gray

You might be in a position where you do a great job and are well liked. You also might have a position that is above theirs and they want to prove that they are superior to you. Also, they may be jealous of your life. There is a reason that they see you as a threat. This does not mean that you are physically or mentally threatening them. They see you as a threat to them and their position in the organisation and the adoration and control they want.

For me, one of the most profound attacks cut into my soul and who I am. This attack come into my life was when I reported a behaviour I did not like to my manager. A colleague was caught unawares and did not like what happened as they did not have control over the situation. From then on, there was a war against me: the lies began, I was isolated by the team, people were turned against me, the boss was used as a weapon to enforce the lies against me and to get me to do things for my colleague. The person's deep need to control to feel safe meant they were prepared to do anything to get back the feeling of safety again. Even if that meant destroying me. The damage that is done in a workplace from bullying and toxic behaviour is huge, both to the employees and to the workplace.

For me, the impact on my life was huge. At that stage, I did not love myself or feel worthy and this questioned every part of me. Going to work every day knowing lies had been told about me was extremely hard. I did not know what the lies were. Trying to achieve and complete my work with my identity and who I was being undermined was a hard road. I tried to come to the workplace cheerful and not let what they said and did bother me. There were other people who knew this person's personality and the tactics; this helped knowing it was more about the other person than me. But it sucked on a major level, tiptoeing around so as not to upset the person, doing what they wanted. So much so it gave this person a lot of confidence knowing they could walk over me and all they had to do was go through the boss to get me to do work for them and get what they wanted.

With bullying, there is a constant behaviour towards you; it is not once off but continual. Being told constantly that you are the problem and that the issue is caused by you and putting you down with other comments does affect you and how you think about yourself.

With these personal attacks, I questioned my identity of who I was. Being cast into the "bad" person role was difficult when I was always the good person who did the right thing, put other people first, and always completed the work. Little did I realise at the time; I am neither the good nor the bad person. I am me and I had to stop taking on the role of the bad person that they assigned to me. I was shaken to the core. Ultimately, I left the position feeling very bitter and angry. Once I left, I made a decision that I was not going to be bitter. I am happy I made this decision, but this took many months before I was able to let go of the bitterness. To remain bitter meant I carried the poison of what they did in me. I spent time making a conscious effort to let go.

Prior to leaving I sought professional help with these issues. Some were helpful and others were not. I remember one telling me that they had to make sure I was not acting like a victim. Sorry, but I was the victim of a systemic attack. Also, how does one not act like a victim? **No helpful information there!**

Once I left, I sought more help to deal with this and another professional helped point out my childhood patterns and because of my perfectionism I was the biggest bully to myself. Ouch did that hurt. I held myself up to these very high standards in my behaviour and I also believed if anyone was upset with me it was my fault. I took the blame for everything that had happened to me. It was not all my fault. The fact it happened was not my fault. How I dealt with it and not putting in boundaries was on me. I am not responsible for other people putting their own shit on me. It is their shit, **NOT MINE**. Part of my upbringing was not to be angry or take it out on someone else.

These unhealthy patterns in my life were like a beacon of light to the bullies to enable them to get what they wanted out of me and I always complied. I often ask myself why I complied; was it the fact that it was fearful for me to speak up or did I not feel worthy to ask for what I wanted and needed? As a child, I felt I was being made fun of what I did, how I spoke, and who I was and the need to be loved meant I learned to do what people wanted from me. The fear from these attacks was huge as if I made moves against them or stood up for myself, the attack would have been even fiercer as they are so used to you obeying them. What they wanted from me was to conform to what they wanted so they did not feel threatened by me and I did not shine any light from myself.

Being on the end of gaslighting left me with a lot of doubts of who I was and what my abilities were. With gaslighting, it is a slow undermining of me by the other person. To know I was being slowly undermined as to my skills and ability to do my job made sense to me as it explained what was going on. I felt horrified knowing someone was deliberately doing this manipulation to me. Looking back over conversations at the constant trivialisation of what I thought, felt, and said, I felt empty inside. I was trying to have a professional relationship with the person, but they were not interested; it was a one-way street in their favour. Anything I brought up was dismissed and I felt rejected as a human being and an employee.

With the bullying behaviour, it is often about having in control and one way to maintain control is instilling fear in the victim. I was living in fear of the person; their ability to maintain their authority and lack of care for me as an individual was devastating. Here was the person that human resources advised me to talk to, but they showed little empathy or compassion for me when I was upset. The tone was completely cold, and they ignored and brushed me off and showed more concern about the business and what work needed to be done. I work in a workplace as a human being not a robot. Work is full of humans, and we all need connection and positive relationships in the workplace.

Is having employees in fear a good approach? The vibe of fear is felt in the business and also by the customers. I remember one place where I visited, when asking for help from a different person, you were referred back to the original person who had helped you. This was frustrating as you either had to wait or leave as you could not get service. This did not make for a healthy vibe when people walked into this workplace and customers knew this did not feel good when they went there.

Unfortunately, I had a few experiences in the workplace where the other person involved ignored what I wanted or what I felt and was more concerned about the business. On one occasion, I practised and had courage to express how I felt. Then I was told that they would take this on board (another word for I will ignore this) and then went straight on to when are you going to get your work done. Somehow, employees are secondary to the business but without the employees there is no business. Humans matter and I remember one department I worked in, there were a couple of managers who lived with the principle that people, and their families, mattered first, business was second. This approach was so nice as the external customers were valued and put first as well. It certainly made a positive difference in that department and to the employees who worked there as it was operated from the heart.

I don't know how some people have lost the perspective of treating their employees as human beings as when employees are supported and encouraged their productivity goes up and the work is completed to a high standard.

> ***Employees who work under great leaders tend to be happier, more productive and more connected to their organization – and this has a ripple effect that reaches your business's bottom line*—Skye Schooley.**

In the past, I have worked on myself and my reactions and knew that it was the other person in one of my workplaces that was bullying and gaslighting me. I had some boundaries but I struggled to talk up. Even if I did in this case, it would not have made a difference as the person was truly committed to feeling in control. Any action of my behalf was met with force to ensure that they had control. They had the ability to put fear into people and made sure people knew of the consequences of not doing what they were told. I felt this workplace was like being back at high school and being bounced around by the school principal. I felt all my knowledge and skills and wisdom were wiped away as only person, the school principal, knew best.

With toxic behaviour in the workplace, none of this is in isolation. You could say, Elizabeth, you are highly sensitive, and you are overreacting to what they said. It was trivial.

They did not mean it. Usually, it is not a single incident, there are multiple incidents built over time. Also, there is never one victim at a time; there are multiple people going through the toxic behaviour. In the situations where I have been bullied, so have other people in the team. In two of my jobs, the person before me left or got another position in another department because of the bullying behaviour. The toxic behaviour leaves multiple victims and a trail and is often known in a company but is not dealt with. Sometimes management is oblivious to the bullying but the employees in a team generally know about it. The people being bullied will leave the workplace and get another job and will give another reason rather than tell the real reason.

It costs very little to say to a person, I hear what you are saying. I am sorry that you are upset. Try putting yourself in their shoes and show empathy.

Another thing I found with the bullying and toxic behaviour was the high level of deflection, away from them and on to yourself. The deflection is that you are the problem, or you did something wrong. During these times, the person seldom apologises and rarely says that they have done something wrong. It is all about pointing the finger at you. Often when a victim of bullying leaves the company and there is a perception that there are no more problems, the assumption is the victim was the problem. Instead, the bullying behaviour remains in the company and this behaviour may or may not be seen again until the person with the bullying behaviours feels threatened by someone else.

I found myself in a better position mentally in respect of knowing my value and that I was worthy. However, the bullying did play on my mind sometimes.

One of more painful episodes was when I was really upset and felt like what had happened was a kick in my guts. I had put off a meeting as I was upset and got messages later, possibly four to five hours later in the day, "Are you ready to talk?" Note the message was not "Are you okay?" You could feel the impatience of the person involved. I told them what I felt, which they ignored. There was absolutely no concern about me, and they were more concerned about themselves and telling me what was going to happen next.

One of the things that I have found is that often there is something about you that they feel threatened by and then they project their insecurities on to you. If they did not feel threatened, they would not behave in this manner. It could be your skills and knowledge, your kindness, you may know the boss well and get on with lots of people. Another experience, I had, was when a new person started and they way the team worked before was changed. A few people in the business said to me that they must have felt threatened by me.

How incredibly sad is this? I was bullied because of someone's insecurity and there is damage to me and to them. Those with bullying behaviours don't realise that they are damaging themselves in the process by their need to feel safe.

Shame

"Shame is a painful feeling that's a mix of regret, self-hate, and dishonor."[25]

Shaming is one of the lowest emotions on the vibration perspective. Usually, shame is when you violate social norms or have a moral transgression. Shame is about you as a person, i.e., viewing that there is something wrong with you, whereas guilt is a behaviour, i.e. I did something wrong.

With bullying, shame is often used to control you and often you are made to feel that there is something wrong with you and you did not meet the social norms of obeying the authority figure.

Writing a new story

Been bullied was a horrific experience for me and I don't want the rest of my life's story to be about a victim of bullying. I don't want to be stuck in this way of being and continually being reactionary to bullying behaviour. I want to change the story and meaning from victim to survivor to thriving. To change and write my new story, one of success and meaning, I need to look at the lessons the bullying behaviour was teaching me and investigate the deep wounds inside of me that were not healed. All of us need to take note of what we are being shown otherwise the lessons will continue. The lessons start out with gentle taps and then get louder until we take note of these lessons. I have had enough of the bullying type of lessons, so I am listening, learning, and healing. Out of challenges and adversity a silver lining is created, and it is God's way to pushing us towards to where our purpose is.

---

[25] vocabulary.com, https://www.vocabulary.com/dictionary/shame

Life is full of challenges and obstacles, and we need to face and deal with them and not run from them. No one is exempt from these challenges, including the person with the bullying behaviour. We need to stop and be still and listen and learn from them. These lessons are our opportunity to grow.

Later on in the book, I will detail my lessons and learning experiences and how I healed from the experiences.

*You've got a new story to write.
And it looks nothing like your past*
—Unknown.

Standing on the Edge

Standing on the edge
The deep unknown waters are below
You breathe in and out
Panic rises up within you
As does the fear
The fear of failure appears so high on the horizon
The fear of being made fun of for following your dreams
You know in your heart you must take flight
To find those 20 seconds of courage
But still the fear rises again
You remind yourself that your work is needed
To share your story to help others
Knowing deep inside that you will be fulfilled

Still you hesitate
Allowing the disbelief of your ability to rise
You tell yourself others are worthy of this but not you
The fight continues inside
Do I or don't I take the plunge
The pain inside is too much
The pain of not doing will be greater than doing
Still you stand on the edge
Finally you decide that you must take that step
Away from the edge
And into the unknown
You close your eyes
You breathe and surrender to God
And step into the air
Down you fall towards those deep waters

Silent No More

You begin to flap your wings
The flight path is messy as you learn to use your wings
You begin to soar and fly higher
You know this is where you are meant to be

Elizabeth Gray 2020

Chapter 7

Impacts Of Bullying

There are many lasting impacts on someone who has been bullied and gaslighted and these include financial, mental, and physical effects. Some people never recover from what has happened to them; others remain stuck in the trauma and this affects their future; and others recover and move on. I have found that sometimes when you think you are healed, thoughts and anger come up and you relive what has happened. The emotional hook can still exist as there are many things to heal.

Writing this book has been challenging as it has brought up many things that happened to me, including being in fear, the injustice of the situation, that I was not seen, heard, and feelings of not being good enough. Out of this experience, I want my voice heard as it has been denied so many times and I felt companies would rather employees be silent than have a voice. I want people to know what bullying behaviour does to people and the effects, I don't want it washed away as an inconvenient truth of what I thought and felt. It mattered to me and I matter.

The most precious gift you can ever give someone is that they are seen, heard, and understood. It does not take too much to really listen to someone. Sometimes they are not asking you to agree with them but to understand what they feel and think. Dismissing someone and their thoughts and feelings is very hurtful.

Anger and bitterness

Coming out of toxic behaviour in the workplace, there are huge feelings of anger and bitterness. The situation was not of my making as the person was determined to get their own way and if I stood up, I was to be quashed.

Elizabeth Gray

One workplace experience left me feeling angry; there is so much anger at the experience, anger at the bully, anger at the company that failed to manage legal requirements such as psychological safety, everyone that wanted to maintain the status quo, anger at myself for not being able to stop this, that the end was extremely messy.

I tried to get the situation resolved; however, if someone is not prepared to meet you in the middle and truly listen it is not possible. I had worked many years and have always tried to create great work relationships but have not been able to do so with someone that did not want a professional relationship. They only wanted a relationship that worked for them and not for both of the people in the relationship. With the bullying and gaslighting, you try and talk up, but others are not interested and keep pushing back to talk with the person that you have the issue with. The power that this person held was significant and they were able to influence others to their way.

Choosing not to be bitter is a decision I needed to make. To overcome bitterness takes an effort on your own behalf as it does take time. It is an important decision to make otherwise it will hold you back and hurt you and not the other people. Withholding forgiveness harms you and not the other person. The quote about drinking poison and waiting for the other person to die is so true as we are holding the poison, not the other person.

> ***Bitterness is like drinking poison and waiting for the other person to die***
> ***—Possibly Buddha.***

Financial, mental, and physical health

In the situations where I was bullied, I had to make decisions based on my physical and mental health and the financial considerations were secondary. When you are so far down the path into the middle of the bullying, it is very hard to make good decisions for yourself. I wanted to make logical decisions and have no emotions attached to them. I wanted to make decisions for myself and not have them forced on me by the person with the bullying behaviour. In many situations, it is not possible as emotions are high and ill health affects the making of logical decisions. In one case, I was able to take time out and recover but still the bullying caused me to quit my job.

Another consideration was the medical aspects of what I was going through. To continue working would have been detrimental to my well-being. To leave would be a cost to my financial situation. Another choice was to leave and play nice or express my truth. Often leaving and playing nice was my default position. I had a policy of not providing exit interviews as I believed these were pointless and nothing is ever done from them. At one place I worked at, it took five years after I left for something to be done about the person's behaviour. The people that came after me had the same problems as me and also left.

Being bullied and having constant stress can have serious impacts on the physical health of a person. These impacts can take time to heal.

My journey to heal has taken a long time after the multiple bullying experiences.

The after-effects

There are massive after-effects; it is not as simple as letting go and moving on. How I wish it was that simple. There is trauma to be healed from. There is your physical health. Not being able to resolve issues at work did not help either. The physical toil on my health was huge as my body got more and more fatigued. The mental aspect was hard. You wish you were not affected by it. Even after you leave, you question yourself, have conversations with the relevant party in your head trying to be heard and get them to understand the impact on yourself. The gaslighting was the worst as you doubt yourself and your abilities.

With bullying, the brain changes as the brain is always on alert to keep you safe and with bullying it becomes alert all the time learning for the next attack on it. "... there are long-lasting chemical and structural brain changes from bullying that account for the cognitive and emotional damage that can be as severe as the harm done by child abuse".[26]

"Bullying is an attempt to instill fear and self-loathing. Being the repetitive target of bullying damages your ability to view yourself as a desirable, capable and effective individual."[27]

"There are two ugly outcomes that stem from learning to view yourself as a less-than-desirable, incapable individual. The first ugly outcome is that it becomes more likely that you will become increasingly susceptible to becoming depressed and/

---

[26] Parker, Warrington S and Brenda A. The Bullied Mind, brainworldmagazine.com, https://brainworldmagazine.com/the-bullied-mind, April 6, 2019
[27] The Long-Term Effects of Bullying, mentalhelp.net, https://www.mentalhelp.net/abuse/long-term-effects-of-bullying

or angry and/or bitter. Being bullied teaches you that you are undesirable, that you are not safe in the world, and (when it is dished out by forces that are physically superior to yourself) that you are relatively powerless to defend yourself. When you are forced, again and again, to contemplate your relative lack of control over the bullying process, you are being set up for Learned Helplessness (e.g. where you come to believe that you can't do anything to change your ugly situation even if that isn't true), which in turn sets you up for hopelessness and depression."[28]

"At the same time, you may be learning that you are helpless and hopeless, you are also learning how you are seen by bullies, which is to say, you are learning that you are seen by others as weak, pathetic, and a loser. And, by virtue of the way that identity tends to work, you are being set up to believe that these things the bullies are saying about you are true."[29] "... bullying included the spreading of rumours and repeated insults aimed at changing the image of the victim and resulting in feelings of guilt, shame and diminishing self-esteem"[30]

What I felt. Rejection, dismissal, nothing. Felt lied about. Bitter. I felt disappointed that the workplace had let me down. How my hopes of being of service and helping others in the business were gone. It was the one part of my job that I really enjoyed, solving problems and training people. Finding my job more limited every day. Having a breakdown in my workplaces with my relationship with my manager. You go to work and

---

[28] The Long-Term Effects of Bullying, mentalhelp.net, https://www.mentalhelp.net/abuse/long-term-effects-of-bullying

[29] The Long-Term Effects of Bullying, mentalhelp.net, https://www.mentalhelp.net/abuse/long-term-effects-of-bullying

[30] Does Workplace Bullying Have Long Term Effects?, tapintosafety.com.au, https://tapintosafety.com.au/does-workplace-bullying-have-long-term-effects/

do your job and then come home. No drama was needed or required. Not feeling able to perform my work as I lost track of what my job was with all the changes going on and work taken off me.

Having worked hard on relationships with everyone and trying to make one with someone who did not want a relationship that worked. The only relationship was that the manager told me what to do. There was nothing co-operative in the process of working together. Even the time spent together in catchups were all about questions being asked. Basically, what was being asked was not that objectionable but the way it was done you felt like you were back in school being addressed by the principal.

Any work that was done before with putting our clients first was washed away. The authoritarian management at one workplace with the determinations of what was going to happen. All the skills and knowledge that we had was wiped away. No one wanted to listen to our opinions and knowledge. It was all wiped away. I found this very soul destroying and the interactions with our internal customers was that we were being told what to do. There was no resemblance of working together. Any change we were told what to think and do and there were not healthy discussions. When you have worked for a long time, this was incredibly soul destroying. I, as a human being, did not matter. I was there as a robot to do what was required. How does that really work for a company?

I lost myself there as what I enjoyed doing was less and less and more mundane work. Trying to have conversations regarding my work really did not work for me. The truly listening and understanding did not exist, it was always about someone else. To achieve anything, you need people working together in a team and not as individuals. To me, I had to pick up after everyone else. And whatever was on their mind that needed to be done. The whole thing was done in contrary to the policies of the company, and these were on paper and not in the hearts of the managers and leaders. And they did not care.

Going through bullying experiences and gaslighting has had long-term impacts on my health, both mentally and physically. The interactions with people that have bullying behaviour plays with your mind, bringing up doubts and not trusting yourself or your abilities. The undermining of you by this behaviour is done through lies, and part truths. You start to doubt what happened to you due to the manipulation of events. When this behaviour is foreign to you, it is hard to see it even when you are experiencing it.

In one company I worked for, my manager told the general manager I did not know how to do my job and who suggested to me that I take two days off during the week and then come on the weekend to learn my job. Was there a manual? NO. Was there help from my manager? NO. So how was I supposed to learn? Ultimately, anything I was not sure of was due to not being able to seek help from my manager and being expected to know the job without being fully trained.

One of the things you suspect but you don't know what is being told about you. Are you now the problem employee or are you incompetent and can't do your job? Have others been told you have a mental problem and can't cope with your job or the work expectations?

There is a lot of deflection on you, that you are the problem. Bullying and gaslighting is very manipulative and they can see what they can do to manipulate you, so they control you. The very undermining of you as a person as long as they get their own way. None of these people ever take responsibility for themselves and their actions. They are too busy pushing everything back on you. That you are completely and utterly at fault. Being blamed and shamed: look at you, you are incompetent, you can't deal with this. When you are a nice person and usually giving this strikes so deep into your heart and psyche. When you have issues with rejection as a child this really is deep and needs to be healed. The blame game is all on you, i.e., you are at fault, no one else. They really know how to put the blame on you. The constant hearing that you are at fault or you did not act properly, or you did not do this, or you reacted. Gaslighting through trivialisation of what you felt and thought is horrendous. You are constantly being dismissed as a person.

I think one of the lasting impacts is the lack of justice around what has happened to you. There seems no path to get justice. Going the legal way is time specific and costs money and you need to be mentally fit to manage this. Usually, you are still suffering trauma and trying to heal and are not in a position to do something about this. Sometimes you are so physically sick that you can't deal with it and have to get out of the company. This means you are not in the position to make the best financial, emotional, and physical solutions for yourself.

The fact you have had to leave, surrender a job you may have loved, your colleagues, your relationships with others because of one person who was determined to have their own way. The fact you were not able to address the issues in the workplace. This is all too common, where the person has to leave and there is no justice. The bully still gets their own way and keeps on working. In many situations, the person with the bullying behaviour gets promoted.

The lack of full perspective from management/human resources in dealing with this is that they don't ask the rest of the team. Too often the bullying is not targeting one person but targeting many in the department. At one place I worked at, the bully became friends with most of the team and one night when we were working back, and I packed up to go home, downstairs was most of the team waiting for that person to go out to dinner which I was not invited to. Not sure why they saw me as a threat; they were more qualified and had more experience than me.

Somehow inside of us, we want justice for what has happened to us. We don't want this to happen to others but when we are still healing it is hard to do that. The purpose of this book is to show what bullying is in the workplace and how it impacts us. I remember speaking to someone that worked in a professional health capacity and I was not their patient and they told me that I had to ring my previous employer and tell them what had happened so it could be prevented being done to someone else. To be asked to do that when I was not healed was extraordinary. Also, what is not understood, often the person complaining is not believed and put down as being vengeful and sour grapes as to what happened. This makes it difficult.

Companies need to know that bullying does not happen in isolation, and it is happening to others in the company. Often a bully gets bullied by another bully and leaves. I have seen this twice in my work experience. However, it leaves another person with the bullying behaviour still there. How do people speak up and be listened to? Do you take part in the exit process and still nothing happens in the company?

Often by the time you leave, you have no trust in the company, management, and human resources to do something about the bullying. Lack of justice can leave you sour and full of bitterness. Wishing for justice and vengeance. A one workplace, I still want some justice for my lost job, for the lies told about me, for management wanting to put me in the same room with my abuser and letting the abuser run the meeting. The unfairness of not having an even playing field. I think management with their processes makes them feel comfortable that they have done the right thing, but they don't consider people's feelings.

There should be a process where everyone can be heard evenly instead of the management making proclamations that they are right, and the employee is wrong. The feeling of helplessness that you are not considered a person but something that needs to go through a process without compassion and empathy. I am not a robot or something that needs to be ticked off on paper that we have done the process correctly. Most of all I think the processes ignore that there is a human being there. One who is worthy of being truly seen and listened to and understood. The lack of being seen and having pronouncements made over you as if you don't exist as a person is extremely hurtful.

Getting another job when we have doubts is really hard. The first job back after a major bullying incident was hard as I had to tell myself I could do this. I had to watch I did not go back into behaviour that did not serve me and act like the victim. It was so hard, but I did it, but it took me time to heal. I did not feel normal until 18 months to two years after that. I was constantly on alert for bullying behaviour.

Why still after that time do I feel I get the blame? It was their bad behaviour, not mine; I will own I was not strong with my boundaries, but they also didn't own their own boundaries.

People make the comment, just get over it but it is not that easy due to trauma bonding. Bullying and gaslighting strike at the heart of a person with all the lies. We have to work out how to make us stronger.

Work through your feelings; it's one of the things you need to do. Feel your feelings; it's okay and don't ever feel ashamed that you struggled with it. Remember that person with the bullying behaviour has enormous experience with this behaviour and winning. Sometimes the days are okay and you're really strong and some days are not okay, you're not strong, you feel really weak and you want to cry. Other days, you're angry, and find it hard to let it go. Really, it comes down to forgiving and letting go and sometimes it's hard work because we really have to work through our triggers that are underneath, i.e., having lack of self-worth.

I made the decision that I will survive, and I'll go on to thrive. I'm not just going to be a victim. I'm going to find my voice and I am tired of being silenced by people. Absolutely tired of it, I've got my voice, I'm going to express what I feel, as what I says matters.

There is something inside that's made us who we are; we are still kind and caring, we are still amazing, giving, and still have so much light in us. Let's not let the darkness of the bullying situations invade our lives. We need to keep the little bright light burning inside. Keep it burning inside and keep fuelling the fire. Focus on the good and on your pure light; how amazing it is that you put out your gift to the world and don't allow them to steal this from you.

*I am not what happened to me.
I am what I choose to become*
—C.J. Jung.

Past, Present, Future

Why do we look
So much back into the past
Of what happened
And why
Wishing things were different
It is called the past for a reason
Take the lessons
Move into the present
Create joy in the moment
Plan and work towards the future
Bringing hope and new possibilities
Of something so much better
Focus on what is ahead
Create the life you want and deserve

Elizabeth Gray 2020

Chapter 8

Justice/Redress

To help victims of bullying behaviour return to a more normal life redress needs to happen but too often this does not happen. Redress will mean to a victim to confirm that they are right and are not to blame and help relieve their shameful feelings.

Wanting justice for what has gone on is natural, but this is one of the areas I have found the hardest to deal. I felt like I was so wronged, and nobody wanted to listen. I felt I talked and talked, and no one listened or understood; sometimes you have to wonder where the line is between standing up for yourself and getting justice or having the stories remain in your brain doing damage to yourself.

Sometimes you have to let go and let God take care of the justice. It is hard as it all seems unfair as nothing has changed for the person who did the bullying whereas you have had your life turned upside down, possibly with ill health and no job or income. I also have another way of looking at things: a person can't put out so much bad stuff and not get any of that back at some time in their life. Also, the other person still needs to learn their lessons. Is that karma? Maybe.

Also have to remind myself what I gained from various experiences that I had. My life and journey are now different, and I am doing what I am supposed to do.

Some bullying can be seen in black-and-white terms and this is usually with other people present who witness the behaviour and report it and the employee is supported. If people were really interested in solving the issues, then they would listen and truly understand the employee before they managed the employee. If there is mutual respect and working towards a solution none of the other stuff needs to happen.

Elizabeth Gray

Going to court or any other legal process is complex and has its own rules. It can come down to proof and often it is shades of grey and not black and white. Court is an adversarial process where each side presents their case and the victim is questioned by the opposing party. This may lead to the victim being traumatised again by the process. I remember going for a job interview and being questioned why I left a particular job, and this brought back the memories and I felt like I was back at work again. This is one of the reasons why deciding to leave and move on can often be the best solution although it does not appear to be at the time. If you do decide to go to court, it may take some time for the case to be heard and legal costs can be huge. Your journey will be what you feel you want to do and what is best for you. Take time out to consider what you want to do. Feel into the intuition for the journey that is right for you.

People can believe that going to court will give them justice and can be disappointed if the result does not go their way. Often this comes down to proof and this is often hard to get it. This is another element of grief that must be gone through. You often feel like it is unresolved.

We have to stop expecting that these people will do the right thing as this is not possible for them. As empaths we like to think that people are good people or people possible of change when they are not. They have no intention of meeting us in the middle and doing the right thing. They need control or energy from you. We have to acknowledge who they are and that they will continue to do the wrong thing by us, and this may never change.

Talking to management about the issues

Solving the issues within the company will depend on how open management and human resources are to listening and understanding before they make a decision. Some questions to consider when you are in the meeting are below:

- Are they seeing me?
- Are they listening to me?
- Are they understanding what I am saying?[31]

Unfortunately, quite often when you are in the middle of bullying, you are emotional and upset and this often makes it more difficult to talk to management. It can be hard to be able to view what happened in a logical manner and you need to concentrate on presenting the facts. Take in a support person with you to help you. Most companies seem to have a policy of a support person who can't talk on your behalf, and they must remain silent. This makes it difficult if there is a power imbalance, and why can't you have a representative in the meeting that can talk on your behalf?

When you want to solve the issues, you are wanting to meet the people with an expectation that it will be resolved in an amicable, reasonable matter. However, if there is narcissistic behaviour involved, this generally will not happen as they will be about defending themselves and putting the blame on to you. It is extremely unlikely you can solve the issues in a reasonable way.

---

[31] Oprah Winfrey, The Oprah Winfrey Show Finale, oprah.com https://www.oprah.com/oprahshow/the-oprah-winfrey-show-finale_1/7, page 7

Non-disclosure agreements

In some cases, there may be a payment as a result of what happened. However, this is usually wrapped up in a non-disclosure agreement and this means the bad behaviour stays under wraps. It also means the victim cannot talk about anything that happened; this may impact on their healing. The continual use of non-disclosure agreements means that the issues are never really resolved, and the offender will often still be in the employment and possibly hurting other people.

Burnout

I have suffered from burnout and fatigue and nearly adrenal fatigue. You put so much into your work and achieving and think you have to keep moving forward. Often, we are not taught self-care which is looking after ourselves mentally and physically. Fatigue is very draining, and you have to rest often. Sometimes I would have to rest the entire weekend to have energy to go to work for the week. In one job, I had to take five weeks out to recover to good enough health that I could return to work. Fatigue means you can't do much in your life but rest. Sometimes you have energy to do something, i.e., walk around a shopping centre for a few hours, and then crash for the weekend. People often use the word busy but are we really living the life we want, or have we got the ladder up the wrong wall? It is important we have balance (your version of balance) in the various elements of our lives, e.g. financial, mental, physical, work, spiritual, hobbies, families, etc. Health is one thing we cannot buy back but often it is the one thing we abuse with overwork, lack of sleep, alcohol, and other things.

We are not filling up ourselves and looking after our bodies as we have been taught to give and give and other people take. We need to balance the giving with receiving as the two go together.

Silent No More

There cannot be one without the other. We need to assess our relationships whether work, personal, family to ensure that there is give and take; we don't need to count that it is 50% exactly as sometimes it goes up and down. However, if it is all one-sided then we need to change it and add in boundaries. We need to look at our relationships, so they build us up and not tear us down. Relationships should be win/win.

The cut has been so deep

Sometimes the cut
Has been so deep
That the healing
Takes a long time
Every now and then
The reminder comes back
And so does the pain
Of the past
And the closure
Was not resolved
And the scar is messy
But because of this
Beauty can rise
Kindness will float
To the top
Love will always win
And loving ourself
Is the greatest gift

Elizabeth Gray 2020

Part Three
Fear, Courage, and God

*Life shrinks or expands in
proportion to one's courage*—Anais Nin.

The Dark Storms

Sometimes the dark storms come
And you feel lost
You feel that you cannot overcome this
You wonder why it is happening to you
The waves keep coming and are higher than before
How much more can you take before you break?
Take a pause on thinking and doing
Decide to take a step off society's treadmill of expectations
It is okay to go all inside
To listen to what is best for you
Know that God has control
And the things are happening for you
To learn and grow
To overcome challenges and obstacles
To become who you were meant to be
A shining light to share your wonder

Elizabeth Gray 2020

Chapter 9

Fear/Courage, Grief, Anxiety, and Depression

*Fear defeats more people than any
other one thing in the world*
—Ralph Waldo Emerson.

Remaining silent

Too often we pay the price for being silent; it stops us from moving forward and keeps us stuck. Sometimes when we talk about our issues, other people are not interested in hearing our negative story and what we went through. By going over and over our story, we often wire the negativity into our brain. If we talk more about our feelings rather than the story it can help us identify our emotions. Identifying the emotions such as anger, fear, etc. means we can identify we have a problem and do something about it. Sometimes it is hard to speak up when something is so wrong and there are costs associated with whether we do or don't talk about it. If we do talk up, we can pay the price with our jobs and income.

Facing fear and the unknown

One of the common meanings for fear is false evidence appearing real. I found fear is an interesting little beast where we stop doing things because we are in fear. But what happens if the relationship with your boss or your partner or someone you know is fear-based; you feel the fear of what they are going to try to do to you. They have used intimidation to try and control you, so you do what they want. They are quite brutal with the way they talk to you and attack you to get you submissive.

We need to overcome this fear by having courage to speak up and sometimes when we speak up, we actually fail at that attempt. We can try again, and most reasonable people will understand and change their behaviour. Sometimes people do things and don't realise that they have hurt someone. However, there will be some that will defend themselves and deny the behaviour and put it back on you. I remember a time when I had difficulty with someone's behaviour. They inferred they were right, and they told me that they were sorry I misunderstood. They did not understand it was about how they made me feel rather than what they said and did.

There are a number of different methods to give someone feedback for their behaviour that cover:

- Facts about their behaviour—be specific
- How you felt
- How you want the behaviour to change
- Be sincere
- Allow them a response
- Listen to the person
- Ensure it is a two-way conversation

Don't use a compliment and feedback at the same time, as the receiver will concentrate on the negative feedback not the positive compliment.

Dealing with fear

> *To overcome fear, here's all you have to do: realize the fear is there, and do the action you fear anyway*—**Peter McWilliams.**

One of the best ways of dealing with fear is to acknowledge that you are fearful. What are you afraid of? To help overcome fear, I try and sit with it (holding it and acknowledging it) and then okay, this is what this is. Just go for it. And sometimes that does not happen, and I allow the fear to get the better of me.

Then I go back and try again. The smallest of actions being brave can lead to other actions taking place. Then you need to work through what is causing your fear—is it a belief?—and then you need to resolve the fear, i.e., facing your fears or journaling them out.

Fear has kept me back a long time from doing things. Fear of doing things I enjoy—crazy and nuts, it is. Too often we are more fearful of success than failure.

Failure—fail early, fail often, fail forward—John Maxwell.

We allow fear to rule us and allow people to put fear into us to stop us from speaking up. We allow the prospect of being laughed at (I know that is one of mine) or made a fool of. I remember learning to ride a bicycle as a teenager and the neighbours over the road were laughing at my attempt. I was determined and at the end of the day I was able to ride the bicycle. Babies are not too scared to learn how to walk and talk and they persist despite being messy and not perfect.

We cannot allow perfection to stop us from achieving. Malcolm Gladwell's book Outliers says it takes 10,000 hours to get to world class. Michael Jordan kept practising, as have so many sportsmen and women. We need to face our fears and do the work anyway. Nobody has started off perfect; look how actors have developed their skills over time.

Sometimes we need to take a very small step and keep doing lots of them. For me putting my poetry out on Instagram was a small start and then I consistently did it. Some days were better than others, but still I kept posting.

> *My philosophy is: It's none of my business what people say of me and think of me. I am what I am, and I do what I do. I expect nothing and accept everything. And it makes life so much easier*—Anthony Hopkins.

> *The cave you fear to enter holds the treasure you seek*—Joseph Campbell.

Overcoming fear is the entry price to the next level and we must embrace it. It is not as bad as we imagine, so give it a go. You have much more to gain than lose.

I think of the quote "What someone thinks of us is none of our business." We need to adopt this approach. Not always to do this arrogantly as sometimes we need to be told when we get out of control. Keeping our plans to ourselves is sometimes good. Do the little steps in secret. If someone laughs at you, have they been brave? We must trust what our journey is meant to be and take those steps. As I said I lived in fear for a long time and was afraid to take action. I was stuck in learning mode for so many years.

It is important that you don't compare yourself with anyone as we all have our unique journey. We have different times to do things in our life. Sometimes as young, others in the middle, and others later in life. Colonel Sanders was 66 years old and had retired when he started Kentucky Fried Chicken. Grandma Moses from the USA did not start painting until she was 76. Frank McCourt wrote *Angela's Ashes* at age 65.

Courage

*Courage is resistance to fear, mastery of fear—not absence of fear—*Mark Twain.

Courage is working through the fear and doing things in the face of fear. For so many years I was paralysed by fear. I think fear of judgement and being made fun of was from a wound a long time ago. For me taking the step of speaking up about the bullying and taking a stand against this type of behaviour is having courage. I look back at my life and there were times when I was courageous, but I have discounted what I have done in the past. Begin with little steps and as they grow so will your confidence. I feel nervous with doing videos on Instagram and Facebook. So, I do prerecord and put it out there, but I need to do more of these. I have to remind myself that it is okay to be messy and imperfect and it is okay to fail. It is okay to suck at doing things. No one starts off perfect.

*Success is the sum of small efforts—repeated day in and day out—*Robert Collier.

Courage is about doing things in fear despite feeling being fearful of what people will say or what the result could possibly be. Take time and face those fears and then take action. Sometimes it's very scary to find our voice to ask people for help or say to people that their behaviour is unacceptable.

It takes courage to grow up and become who you really are—E.E. Cummings.

*Inaction breeds doubt and fear. Action breeds confidence and courage. If you want to conquer fear, do not sit home and think about it. Go out and get busy—*Dale Carnegie.

Grief

I went through a process of grief when I left one of my jobs. Even though I pulled the plug on my job, I felt like I had no choice as I needed to survive and move on. As part of the healing, I have had to go through a grieving process. When we go through the processes of what we did and what happened to us. We actually need to grieve because there a number of losses including with loss of job, loss of income and even our identity. These losses can impact your relationships with your family and others and lead to further losses. Elisabeth Kűbler Ross describes the seven stages of grief:

- Shock and disbelief
- Denial
- Guilt
- Anger and bargaining
- Depression, loneliness, and reflection
- Reconstruction and working through
- Acceptance and hope[32]

We have to give ourselves time to work through these processes and acknowledge and ask for assistance if we have stayed in these processes too long. You are allowed to grieve; don't let anybody tell you otherwise or when or how your response should be.

Sometimes the feelings are so intense and even if we understand the logic, it is hard because the emotion is overwhelming. We have to deal with the emotion first, often by sitting with it and

---

[32] The 5 (or 7) stages of grief & loss: Grief cycle and grieving process, proactivemindfulness.com, https://www.proactivemindfulness.com/grief-stages/

acknowledging it before it can leave us, and then we can tackle the logic.

Anger is one of the main components you feel after you have been bullied. It can last a long time because there is often no justice or redress for the situation, especially if you lose your job or income from it. Anger is part of the grieving process. Anger can affect your mental and physical health. Going over and over the situation can cause the brain to be wired negatively. Be kind to yourself and forgive yourself as you go through the grieving process. You need to be able to focus on the future and doing things you enjoy.

Anxiety and depression

In dealing with anxiety at work, the rise of the anxiety usually happened in a certain location while I was on the bus to work, about five to ten minutes after catching the bus. It was down the hill in Marshall Road towards the busway which would take me into the city. At that moment dread would come over me and I would feel anxiety. What would happen at work today? Who would attack me? What was I fearing? Not knowing what would be said or done to me. I knew I didn't have any control over what they did and how they acted, and no-one else did either. Often on the bus with my eyes closed I would pray but also do deep breathing, i.e., breathing in love and breathing out love. I slowed my breath right down and this helped ease some of the anxiety. I made a conscious effort to go into the office to be very upbeat and not let people see that I was upset by what they were doing. At one stage, I took some natural medicine to help with symptoms of anxiety. Another recent symptom of anxiety was that I found my heart racing. Again, slowing down my breath helped me. I had become very anxious during COVID-19. When my physical health goes down, this has a huge impact on my mental health.

Elizabeth Gray

I have suffered from depression a number of times and for me depression is a loss of hope for the future and not believing anything good is going to happen to me. For others, depression may mean something different. In the bad times I had a lot of negative thinking and this spirals and wires it in your brain. By continually thinking the negative, it is easy to think negative. I thought I was on a hamster wheel and was going around in circles. For many years I did not know how to get off the hamster wheel. At one time, I had a very deep episode of depression, and I had really considered killing myself by jumping off the Victoria Bridge in Brisbane, Queensland. At this stage, I was not physically well as I was not dealing well with the humidity and when my health goes down, the more negative my brain gets. My depression lifted and disappeared, and the only explanation was that it was a gift of grace from God. It just went and I am so grateful that I received a miracle from God. I have had other touches of depression but never like that one.

There are plenty of organisations where you can find help with grief and anxiety and depression. In Australia, there are organisations such as Lifeline, Beyond Blue, RUOK. Get help from someone that understands this and can help you through. Finding the right person to help is important. One who will listen and not judge and especially someone that will help you move forward. I found over time if you keep talking about it, a lot of people back away from you as they don't want to hear the negativity all the time. At times, I have had suggestions like go help other people. A good friend will listen to you in the times you want to rant. For me, having those friends was absolutely necessary to have the support. Also, I went to prayer at the Healing Rooms Australia[33] and also at church.

It is okay to ask for help; we often don't want to bother or burden people with where we are and how we feel. Reaching out for help is a sign of strength. There are lots of people that want to help you. There is no shame in having anxiety and depression. Too often, there is a myth out there about being tough and working through and to ignore your mental and physical pain. This is not healthy and can damage your physical body. To end up coping with the difficult work situations I was in, I had mentally disconnected myself from my body. I told myself that I had to work to make a living and keep a roof over myself. I kept on going and pushing on and going into work situations that were not healthy for me, either mentally or physically. Our body does give us messages, but we tend to push on regardless.

A lot of famous people have had depression; it affects all people and is non-discriminatory. Some of these include Dwayne Johnson (The Rock) and Katy Perry. Some in Australia include ex-politicians like Jeff Kennett, Geoff Gallop, and Malcolm Turnbull.

Suicide

Unfortunately, some victims of bullying commit suicide. The continuing messages of how they are not good enough or they are weak or a failure or they think everyone will be better off without them. I know how low I got when I contemplated committing suicide. I decided I had had enough of this life and all the things that were happening to me. I could not see a way out or anything positive. Fortunately for me, God lifted this

---

[33] https://www.healingrooms.com.au/

Elizabeth Gray

from me but also, I have worked with professionals when I felt in a bad situation and also went for prayer.

If you feel that life is so bad that you are thinking about suicide, please seek professional help.

Don't move the way
Fear makes you move
Move the way
Love makes you move—Rumi.

I Am Here

I am here
I was created by God
I am not an accident
I have come with a purpose
One I need to complete
No one else can do this work
Other than me
No one else can be allowed
To stop me
From my purpose
As it was divinely created
For me

Elizabeth Gray 2020

Chapter 10

Faith And God - Directed Purpose

God is bigger than any problem. God in you is greater than any difficulty you have to meet. God cares for you more than it is possible for any human being to realize. God can help you in proportion to the degree in which you worship him. You worship God by really putting your trust in him instead of in outer conditions, or in fear, or in depression, or in seeming dangers, and so forth. You worship God by recognizing his presence everywhere, in all people and conditions that you meet; and by praying regularly. You pray well when you pray with joy—Emmet Fox.

I have a faith in God, and I refer to God throughout this book. You may instead wish to see where I mention God as Universe, source, spirit or power.

I feel like my journey has been led by God. God has been with me through these difficult moments, and I had faith that good would come out of these experiences. Despite going through horrific experiences, I knew that God was with me. Throughout the resulting trauma of being bullied, I knew God had a plan and I needed to trust it. Knowing and surrendering to God took patience and practice. I was grateful that I was able to see the plan.

The finality accumulated in me leaving one of my jobs by resigning. It felt like I had been hit by a Mack truck and been knocked out of the way of myself. In a way I can see this all being part of God's plan to take me on the path he had created for me. I did have nudges and things whispering through my life, but I did not understand, and I ignored them until it was too late and this experience helped me choose to move away from the safe corporate long term and do what I was meant to do. I realised some time ago that I was in the right place and all that I had experienced had led me to this moment and I felt very peaceful over this. I worked on where I was at. I was so grateful for one of my coaches, as without her I would not have been strong enough to undertake the journey through bullying and gaslighting and not come out of the other side to speak my truth. There are always two sides to a story and meeting in the middle would have been a wonderful outcome for me but that was not meant to happen.

It was time to look after myself instead of others and leave the workforce to get healthy, both mentally and physically. The long physical toll on my body was huge with viruses, allergies, and fatigue. I was wiped out by the process.

I felt God's plan was for me to stop staying in workplaces where I have been bullied and speak up around bullying. Too long have the victims of bullying had to be silent and had to endure extraordinary behaviour from colleagues, managers, and subordinates.

I began to do a Daily OM Memoir Writing Course[34] and part of that course was to write a poem, which is "Silent No More" in this book. After that I kept writing poetry as a release of what I was feeling and then started painting. All of these have led me to come back home to myself, so I am no longer defined by what I experienced and what their version of me was. At some stage, we need to become ourselves, what God created us to be. For so long we follow society's expectations of who we should be, and we forget who we were meant to be, that God created. God has created us individually and has a plan for us to prosper.

---

[34] Write. Heal. Transform: A Magical Memoir-Writing Course, dailyom.com, https://www.dailyom.com/cgi-bin/courses/courseoverview.cgi?cid=915&aff=0#

> "For I know the plans I have for you,"
> declares the Lord, "plans to prosper you
> and not to harm you, plans to give you
> hope and a future"—Jeremiah 29 11[35]

As Cathy Heller said, "We are not created as extras." Even if we change one person's life, we have made a difference. We all have a role to do on earth.

Don't die with the music still in you—Wayne Dyer.

The music is what God has placed in us and we need to play the music; some of us start young, some in the middle, or some later in life. Take comfort and keep working forward to discover your purpose and sometimes this is by doing the work and taking action. Being in the flow is an experience where time vanishes and when you are in the flow you are doing God's work. God created us for so much more than being defined by others; we are meant to work together and bring the best out in others. Often people can see the gems in us more than we can see ourselves. Along the way, we developed baggage such as being not good enough, not worthy, having nothing to offer, and feeling rejected as we are. This is not how God meant us to be.

By writing this book, I have had a knowing that this is the path for me. I have been very mindful of listening to my intuition and following my journey. This is hard to explain but it is feeling that you have peace and are on the right path. In the past, the other shiny object syndrome and women's way of having to keep learning so I am qualified enough. Now, I am listening to the heart (aka God), and it does know where it

---

[35] Biblica, Inc. TM, The Holy Bible, New International Version® NIV®

should go. It does not promise no difficulties on your path or that you don't have to work. It is such a peace and following the path is easier. Doubts still raise their head. Coming into a book writing intensive week[36] where the program is designed to write a book in a week, I felt that I was not good enough to write this book. But deep inside I felt God directing me to get this book out and help others that have been through bullying to recover and heal. Bullying has remained so silent due to fear.

> *Our job is to bring out the work and it is God's job to take it from there*—**Rabbi David Aaron.**

Trusting God that this will happen. Wherever this book goes to and what comes out of it, it is God's choice. Part of my healing is writing this book and being able to put who I am on a page. This book is intended with love and to help others. This book is not intended to shame and blame others. All is intended to highlight the effects of bad behaviour such as bullying in the workplace and the huge cost it is to both employees and the employer and hopefully people will take on and do their healing and those in business will understand the impacts and take action.

Tim Challies[37] spoke in his blog about God's tapestry; this where we only see the back of the rug where all threads are messy, and you can't see the picture unless you look at the front. God is doing the weaving. Sometimes we make it hard for him, but he brings it back to him. All of us have had things that have happened to us and it is how we look at them and

---

[36] Book writing intensive at https://inspirationalbookwriters.com
[37] Challies, Tim. God's Tapestry, challies.com, https://www.challies.com/articles/gods-tapestry/, January 19, 2005

how God uses these things in our lives. Talking about what happened to us can open up things that need to be discussed.

Only recently more people have been speaking up with similar topics like Me Too, sexual harassment, Jeffery Epstein, and the 2021 Australian of the Year Grace Tame speaking up about the sexual abuse by her teacher. By sharing our stories, we can help others through difficult times and also make an impact in stopping bad behaviour. Unfortunately, in a lot of cases, many people have to suffer before they will be believed. We need to stop this and treat people with love as God has loved us. When we leave ego behind and come from a place of love then beautiful things happen. Understand what drives a person; some of their stuff may be hidden and we have to find a way for it to come out in a gentle, loving way, not condemning. When I look back at my times at work, I would have loved to resolve the issue, but I have to accept it wasn't possible.

The best revenge is massive success
—Frank Sinatra.

God is always kind and just. Remembering that God is just, and he is charged of justice means that we can leave it in his hands. Too often we overreact and want to do things to take revenge. The quote, the best form of revenge is success, is the one I like to follow. We do have a choice to heal and come out of bullying. Often, we don't realise that we had a choice as we are too much stuck in the mud fighting to come out.

Doing things out of love is more powerful than doing things out of fear. A meditation I love is the heart brain coherence that leaves me in such a wonderful place of feeling love.

God is love. Trusting God has the best for you and taking the ego out of yourself. It all comes down to trust instead of trying to find our own way and using the ego. Trust is sometimes hard when you are in a difficult financial situation and knowing when you should take action inspired by God and when you should surrender and let go.

Surrendering is such a powerful thing. It is letting go of outcomes and trusting that things will be okay. We often find surrendering hard because our brain and ego gets in the way. Too many times we want to have control. Control over the outcome. Surrendering is trusting God. Without attachment to an outcome, it is easier to allow things to happen.

Prayer is so important; I pray for protection every day from Ephesians and speak *The Lord's Prayer* out loud every day. I also read the Bible every day. Find something that works for you that connects you with your faith and God.

Ephesians 6: The Armor of God

[10] **Finally, be strong in the Lord and in his mighty power.** [11] **Put on the full armor of God, so that you can take your stand against the devil's schemes.** [12] **For our struggle is not against flesh and blood, but against the rulers, against the authorities, against the powers of this dark world and against the spiritual forces of evil in the heavenly realms.** [13] **Therefore put on the full armor of God, so that when the day of evil comes, you may be able to stand your ground, and after you have done everything, to stand.** [14] **Stand firm then, with the belt of truth buckled around**

your waist, with the breastplate of righteousness in place, [15] and with your feet fitted with the readiness that comes from the gospel of peace. [16] In addition to all this, take up the shield of faith, with which you can extinguish all the flaming arrows of the evil one. [17] Take the helmet of salvation and the sword of the Spirit, which is the word of God.[38]

God's purpose is within us and the messages starts off softly and then gets so loud. It seems that we are taught over time to diminish the voice in us. I remember watching a video of Stan Lee and how he created Spiderman and how the publisher said, "Stan, that is the worst idea I have ever heard."[39] In the end Stan Lee put Spiderman on the expected last edition of *Amazing Fantasy* and it made great sales and then it was put in a series. Stan Lee listened to his voice and made it a success.

It's really important that we don't lose hope for that little voice in us; it's telling us we must take this journey. The journey of fulfilment, the journey of being loved, the journey of just being who we're meant to be. By being whom we're meant to be, we can bring so much to the world by putting our story out there and finding our voice. You are letting people know you matter, I matter, and they matter. We need to have that voice where we're not quashed and put down. Too often the voices that are negative are very strong, but we have to empower people and lift them up. If we are living from a true space of love, ego doesn't have a spot in there. It's often our egos that trigger us.

---

[38] Biblica, Inc. TM, The Holy Bible, New International Version® NIV®

[39] Stan Lee on how the idea of #Spiderman was born. Arvind Joshi YouTube channel, May 7, 2019

Elizabeth Gray

***Who are we not to do it and to put ourselves out*—Cathy Heller.**

We were created for a purpose so speak up and find your voice. By speaking up you can help others that have been through a similar story. However, when we offer service—it can be by being a cleaner, working in a bank, writer, artist, engineer, or multimillionaire—we are meant to use our gifts as we're all together on this human journey, helping each other out.

This world is meant to be difficult, and your life on earth is meant to be a struggle, filled with adventure, challenge, and victory. This is your divine mission if you are willing to accept it. And if you accept it, you will have the power to succeed—
Rabbi David Aaron

Part Four
Learning from the Experiences

By three methods we may learn wisdom: first, by reflection, which is noblest; second by imitation, which is easiest; and third by experience, which is the bitterest—Confucius.

The Knowing

The knowing
That you are in the right place
At the right time
The future that you want
Will come to you
Knowing
The pathway
Is being revealed
By the light shining
Through the darkness
Knowing
And trusting God
This is where you are meant to be
To fulfil your purpose
On earth

Elizabeth Gray 2020

Chapter 11

My Healing

When we meet real tragedy in life, we can react in two ways—either by losing hope and falling into self-destructive habits, or by using the challenge to find our inner strength—
Dalai Lama XIV.

Do not look for healing at the feet of those who broke you—Rapi Kaur.

For me, I had to choose to heal. I did not want to go through any bullying experiences again. It was horrific and traumatic to be treated less than a human. I needed to choose what was right for me and no more giving up or contorting myself to please people and to get recognition. I needed to put myself first and fill myself up so I could serve from a full cup. Leaving one of my workplaces was the best thing to stop the drama and have control over my life instead of allowing others to have it.

Along with leaving became a string of losses: loss of my identity, loss of relationships with colleagues, loss of income, loss of good health. Yes, it is good to leave but I had to deal with grief, anxiety, and depression. My journey back to health is taking a long time, both mentally and physically. Part of the healing was letting go of the old identity I had in my job title and position. Who was I in the workplace?

Taking time out from the workplace has been so beneficial as I had needed to heal all my wounds from the past. In a way COVID-19 gave me a cocoon where I could heal. I decided that I was not going to be defined by my work or others' opinions of me and I needed to work forward and become my own hero.

The changing of the mindset takes longer when you are not physically well. Not being physically well enough was making an impact on my mental well-being. The frustration around my health grew and grew as I was not able to do too much other than rest. I had become highly allergic and suffered from constant sinus infections. Trying to let go, trying to find answers and the frustrations grew. A few times along with the way, I had to accept where my health was and let it go and surrender. A friend recommended some tablets to me that have picked up my mental and physical health, but it is still an ongoing journey. I can get very tired and have to rest and pace myself and still watch what I eat.

As part of this journey, I started to write poems for healing and then painting art. I write the poems on what I feel on the day. The process of writing the poetry was being in my flow and writing what I felt helped me heal as I could express what was in my heart. I started painting after doing a small online course. I also spent time doing English Paper Piecing; for those that don't know, it is fabric in shapes like hexagons and triangles and sewn together by hand. I found this process relaxing. Doing things that gave me joy was a priority. For too long I was taught that pain and suffering are the only way ahead. Working and doing what I love is a giant experiment and I needed to be messy and try things out and see what works. Brilliance and expertise do not come at once; it takes many hours. I needed to try and do things and be okay to fail. There is so much emphasis on not failing but failing is important as it can give us guideposts to our next step. Moving forward is the main thing I can do and see what happens.

Healing doesn't mean the damage never existed.
It means the damage no longer controls your life ...
—**Akshay Dubey.**

Healing is a journey and will take time, but **we need to choose** to become healed. Sometimes we think we are over something that happened, a reminder comes up and we think like it was yesterday when it happened. Our body reacts to our thoughts and it does not distinguish whether it is happening now or it happened in our past. Therefore, the constant reliving of your experiences has the same impact on your body that it did at the time those experiences happened. Going over and over what happened in constant conversation either with someone or yourself is not helpful and keeps you stuck in the negative loop.

We need to recognise when our thoughts are not healthy or not useful to us. It takes awareness and practice to keep these thoughts at bay. As with meditation, you can thank your thought and let it pass or you can also say to that thought that you no longer need it. Also, you can write down your thoughts and anger on paper and then you can burn the paper. Find a way so the thoughts are not renting out your brain.

Your value does not decrease based upon someone's inability to see your worth—Anonymous.

THINGS WE CAN DO

Be kind to ourselves
Release the judgement
Of what we did
Or did not do
We are human
We will make mistakes
Be grateful
Focus on the good things
In our lives
Let the problem go
Focus on the solution
Be mindful of our thoughts
Capture them
Dismiss the negative
Maintain the positive
Keep on going
Find the joy in your life

Elizabeth Gray 2020

//
Chapter 12

What Worked For Me

Instead of saying "I'm damaged, I'm broken, I have trust issues" say "I'm healing, I'm rediscovering myself, I'm starting over."
Horation James.

The core things that I did that helped me on my road to healing were:

- Choosing myself over other people and my work situations
- Taking 100% responsibility for myself
- Healing my old wounds from childhood and doing the inner work
- Loving and accepting myself
- Acknowledging my worth and value
- Changing my thinking and believing that good things can happen
- Watching my thoughts and taking action when old thought patterns came up and being mindful of my habits around my thoughts
- Changing my story from victim to thriver

I have found healing is not one thing over the other and have listed the areas below that I focused on. It is important to find what works for you and follow your own path. Find people that you connect with you and bring out the best in you and believe in you. The people that would love you and gently tell you the truth and encourage you.

Professional help

- Seeking professional help from psychologists or counsellor
- Having a coach

If you need help don't hesitate to reach for professional help from your doctor or psychologist or counsellor. There are a number of helplines that can help you. Find someone that really listens to you. One of my favourite counsellors was one I could have a laugh with at what happened to me. I also liked having a coach as they concentrate on moving you towards your goals and future.

What I did for myself

These are some of the things I did for myself:

- Choosing myself first
- Becoming my own hero
- Self-care
- Making decisions to heal
- Making choices
- Being grateful
- Celebrating
- Being my own best friend
- Choosing that I matter
- Following the soul
- Leading from heart and from love
- Loving myself
- Appreciating myself

I chose myself first and made my self-care a priority.

Mindset

Doing the inner work and changing my mindset was one of the most important parts of moving into my future. It is hard work and there is no easy way but the rewards are so amazing. Being aware of my negative thought patterns and habits was very important as is watching what I think. There are so many different processes and I have listed some of the processes that I have used.

- Journaling
- Changing my story
- Doing the inner work
- Healing the childhood wounds
- Doing programs for self-development
- Self-development workshops
- Reading self-development books
- Taking back my power
- Stop playing it safe
- Listening to intuition and not others
- No judgement
- No complaining
- Creating and owning a new identity, i.e., like Beyoncé has Sasha Fierce
- Watching my thoughts
- Doing I AM statements
- Having mantras
- Loving myself
- Accepting and approving of myself
- Forgiving myself
- Loving and accepting my body
- Letting go and surrendering
- Forgiving others
- Letting go of resistance
- Listening to talks on YouTube
- Listening to uplifting Podcasts
- Changing my mindset
- Putting in boundaries
- Talking to friends and others
- Believing in self and the future
- Focusing on the future
- Changing focus
- Using what happened as fuel

Body

Looking after your body should be one of your priorities as without a healthy body it can be hard to think clearly.

It is important to relax your body along with your mind. These are some of things below I did for my mind and body.

- Yoga—Yin and Restorative
- Meditation
- Eating healthy
- Going for walks
- Connecting with nature
- Listening to healing music on YouTube
- Doing healing meditations

Also eating healthy foods is so important and we often use certain types of food and alcohol to medicate us from feeling. Allow yourself to feel your feelings.

Doing things you love

It is incredibly important to do things you enjoy; this helps you get into the flow where you lose the sense of time. Do creative things.

- Writing poetry
- Doing art
- Quilting
- Walks in nature
- Gardening
- Singing
- Dancing
- Exercise
- Travelling

Anything that gives you joy and helps you be in the flow.

Healing processes

- Prayer
- Energy healing
- Tapping
- Emotional releasing techniques

There are a lot of processes that you can use to heal trauma and emotions. Prayer is wonderful and there are healing centres across Australia and churches where you can get prayer.

I have used an energy healer to help me remove stuck emotions. People may disagree with these types of healing but I found these processes beneficial to me. It is your choice about what you feel comfortable with.

I also underwent processes from NLP (neuro-linguistic programming) that helped the emotions that were blocked leave my body.

Healing is layers. Healing is time. Healing is excruciating. Once you think it's done, it's not
—Mary De Muth.

Inner Work

Sitting still
Going deep inside
To ask for help
To hear the tiny whisper
In reply
Sometimes a new revelation
Other times a confirmation
Of what I believed I needed to do
Deep breathe
Take hold of the courage
To take the next small step

Elizabeth Gray 2020

Chapter 13

Doing The Inner Work

> *Don't be distracted by criticism. Remember, the only taste of success some people have is when they take a bite out of you*—Zig Ziglar.

> *To heal a wound you need to stop touching it*—Unknown.

Over time and from events in childhood, we have developed unhealthy habits such as people pleasing, being afraid of conflict, unable to speak our truth and put in healthy boundaries. We also have developed fear around being rejected or criticised if we say something to those people. In essence we hand over our power to the other person and we need to take it back. We have to stop allowing these people to define us and have this behaviour holds us prisoner to them.

Only we can put a meaning to what people say to us based on our behaviours. We have to stop taking on their meaning. If they don't like us or they have an opinion of us that we find upsetting it does not mean that they are correct about what they think. I like the unknown saying, "Don't take criticism from someone that you won't take advice from." So, if you would not go to them for advice, don't take the criticism. Not everyone we meet will support us or be encouraging so we have to make the call about what they say about us and examine whether the criticism is relevant or not.

> *A lot of cheap seats in the arena are filled with people who never venture onto the floor. They just hurl mean-spirited criticisms and put-downs from a safe distance. The problem is, when we stop caring what people think and stop feeling hurt by cruelty, we lose our ability to connect. But when we're defined by what people think, we lose the*

***courage to be vulnerable. Therefore, we need to be selective about the feedback we let into our lives. For me, if you're not in the arena getting your ass kicked, I'm not interested in your feedback*—Brené Brown.**

Old childhood wounds make us sensitive to their criticisms. In life, we will be criticised whether we do things or not. We need to roll with the criticism taking on what is necessary to improve and grow and throw out the rest. Don't let people define us by what they think about us. Also, if we don't believe what they are saying about us it is easier to let go. This is why we have to clear out our childhood wounds as it is easier to dismiss someone when they say we are not good enough when we believe we are good enough.

The inner work, which is working on your mindset, beliefs, and thoughts, is so important. It is a very hard road, but it is worth it.

Think of yourself in 5 or 10-years' time: if you remained the same what will happen, i.e., will you remain broke, unhealthy, working in a soulless job, or what could happen if you changed. For example, you could be working at a job you love that does not feel like work, you are healthy and fit, and having wonderful personal relationships and financial freedom.

Which would you choose to do? You can choose to be successful, but you have to make a commitment to do it until you get there.

We have to ask ourselves better questions. These will help us make better decisions. So, the questions you can ask yourself are:

- What can I do right now that will help me?
- What must I do today?
- What can I say no to?
- How can I let this go?
- What do I need to do next?
- What direction should I take?

When your thoughts go to negative, ask yourself:

- Does this thought belong to me?

This helps you determine whether these negative thoughts come from you or not. Often, we take on a thought and belief that is not ours.

Another set of questions you can ask yourself are from Byron Katie:

1. Is it true?
2. Can you absolutely know that it's true?
3. How do you react when you believe that thought?
4. Who would you be without the thought?[40]

Often, we talk in absolutes, i.e., never or always. These four questions help break through this thinking as it is rare that something always or never happens.

Often, we have resistance to change or things that have happened. Usually whatever we resist often persists and we need to surrender and let go. The more we concentrate on what we don't want the more it will remain. It will overshadow anything else in our lives. It is so easy to get trapped in our stories of what happened. Quite often what

---

[40] Katie, Byron. The Work is a Practice, thework.com, https://thework.com/instruction-the-work-byron-katie/

happened was unfair and we could not get any fairness to happen. Surrendering can be hard, but truly letting go is the best way. Sometimes writing down on paper helps with this.

We need to focus on what we want as whatever we focus on grows. So, if we concentrate and put all our energy into what we want, this will help us succeed.

> ***What you focus on grows, what you think about expands, and what you dwell upon determines your destiny*—Robin Sharma.**

A lot of people have coaches and if you look at the professional athletes, they will have multiple coaches, i.e., one for skill, one for mindset, one for health, etc. Having a coach will help you grow. I have benefited so much from coaches in my life, they have helped me move forward.

Making choices

Make a choice to heal, you can choose how you heal. You have the freedom to choose. Choose to live in the vibration of love which is one of the highest.

Make choices to feel good about yourself. Write positive statements. Write out your new identity (who you want to be) as your own hero and read it every day. Practise mindfulness and meditation.

When you make decisions from a wonderful place like love, these are so much more powerful than making decisions from shame or guilt. Bullying keeps us in the shame/guilt vibration.

Be your own best friend

Take ownership of your relationship with yourself. Stop talking to yourself in an abusive manner and being hard on yourself. Learn to love and appreciate yourself. Treat yourself as your own best friend. What would you say to them, how would you support them? Do this for yourself.

Awareness

Psychologist Nathaniel Branden said, "The **first step** toward **change** is **awareness**. The second **step** is acceptance."

Unless we have awareness around an issue or a behaviour we have, we are unable to change it. Any changes start with awareness and then acceptance and then change. The next step is to take action; without action there is no change.

> *Don't ignore pain; appreciate its message: You need to change now!*—Shannon L. Alder.

Expecting others to change

> *Stop expecting others to act first, be the one who makes a positive change*—Leon Brown.

We have no control over others and often when something happens to us, we want the other person to change their behaviour. However, the only control is we have is to change our own behaviour and that is where we must focus.

When we get triggered by someone's behaviour, there is a gap between being triggered and you have a moment to decide whether you will react or respond. Reacting means allowing your emotions to dictate what happens and this may involve losing your temper, arguing with the person. Responding means talking in a positive way and in some cases your response may be silence.

We need to manage ourselves and our emotions and deal with our own triggers and not the other person's.

Healing our wounds and suffering

> *Pain is inevitable: suffering is optional*—Haruki Murakami.

I had a belief that I had to suffer in life. But it is our choice to suffer or not. When we experience the pain, we often hold on to the pain and go over and over it in our heads and continue to hold on the pain and suffer. Letting go of the pain is healthy and it does take time to do so.

> *The wound is the place where the Light enters you*—Rumi.

If we have pain, we have not fixed our wounds. Often our wounds start in our childhood aged between zero and seven where we place a meaning of what happened and apply it to ourselves. It is often things like I am not worthy, I am not valued. For me one of my wounds I internalised was that I did not matter, and I had to make sure everyone else was more important than myself and my needs.

When we are bullied, the bully will find our unhealed wounds and what we believe about ourselves. This means the pain is so bad and cuts into our soul as our soul believes we are not worthy or not valued.

Without healing our wounds, they still hurt us and we have created stories around them and we continue them into our lives. When these wounds are triggered, we are hurt.

Emotions/triggers/resilience

Awareness is the birthplace of possibility. Everything you want to do, everything you want to be, starts here—Deepak Chopra.

Something will happen or someone says something, and we will get triggered. It could be someone cutting you off in traffic, someone being rude to you, someone yelling at you.

We are all responsible for ourselves and our lives. To understand this is that we are responsible for our reactions and the choices we make in our lives. There will be things out of our control and people will say things to us. But we need to respond and not react and keep going on own journey.

The trigger will be something unresolved pain from your childhood and something you have attached meaning to. Some of the triggers come from the following:

- Rejection
- Shaming
- Being ignored
- Someone controlling you
- Judgement from other people
- Being needy

Some of the emotions that you can feel when you are triggered are:

- Anger
- Sadness
- Shame
- Guilt

The emotions that bullies use to manipulate you include shame, guilt, and blame. We need to heal our childhood wounds. Without this healing we will still continue to react to the bullies.

It is healthy to feel your emotions, name them, and acknowledge them. This way you can work through them. We do have to feel them to let them go in a healthy way. After my father died, I did not experience grief until months later and then I realised I was sad and grieving. I named my feeling as grief and let it be. I did not fight or resist the feeling; after a few days it went away. It did come back again, and I did the same process again.

> ***Between stimulus and response there is a space.***
> ***In that space is our power to choose our response. In our response lies our growth and our freedom***
> ***—Viktor E. Frankl.***

We have to look at the triggers and emotions that we have and find a way to deal with them in a healthy way, otherwise we can have addictions.

One way to change is working out our trigger and replacing the old reaction with a new action.

- Trigger—what upset us
- Current reaction—get angry
- New reaction—go for a walk

When an event happens and you feel bad, there might be something you did not get from the event. What were you looking for respect or acknowledgment? The other party is not able to meet your needs and only you can meet your needs. We have to stop looking at others for validations or significance.

We have to look inside ourselves for our answers and we matter, and we have to choose ourselves. We have stop looking at what people said about us or did to us.

Releasing our emotions

The worse thing we can do is suppress our emotions. This comes at our cost, and this can manifest in our body and can lead to anxiety and depression. The more we resist these emotions the more they will persist. Often, we will turn to food, alcohol, and drugs to moderate our emotions and these are short-term fixes.

We all must find a way to release our emotions.

A process to help deal with your emotions and help them pass through is below:

- Become aware of what your emotions are
- Name your emotions
- Feel your emotions
- Breathe through them
- Thank the emotions and let them pass out of your body and shake your body

Tara Brach's method to deal with emotions is R.A.I.N. process is below:

- Recognize what is happening;
- Allow the experience to be there, just as it is;
- Investigate with interest and care;

- Nurture with self-compassion.[41]

Other ways include talking or writing your emotions out via journaling. Physically crying when you are upset is also a good way as is bashing pillows if you are angry.

No judgement/complaining

Often when we experience traumatic experiences, we talk about them over and over and this creates a negative path in our brain where the thoughts go to the path of least resistance. When you have a negative bias, you subconsciously look for the evidence to prove that was true. What was the last car you bought? Say a blue Ford. Now all of a sudden you only see a blue Ford. They were there before but now you own one you see lots of them.

So, if we believe we are hopeless we look for that evidence. I was looking through all these bullying experiences as evidence I was not good enough and I did not have anything to offer. I knew I had to change what I thought and to stop looking for damming evidence and start looking for evidence that proved positiveness. I started with I AM statements and wrote them out multiple times to help me change the way I thought. Some of the I AM statements were:

I am worthy
I am loved
I am valuable

Try saying something good about yourself and see what comes back. I am worthy of being loved.

---

[41] Brach, Tara. Resources ~ RAIN: Recognize, Allow, Investigate, Nurture, tarabrach.com, https://www.tarabrach.com/rain/

In addition, we have to stop judging ourselves. Too often we put such a high standard on ourselves on how we act and how we should be. We judge ourselves that we are not good enough or what we do is not good enough. Start to catch yourself when you judge yourself and let it go. Also watch yourself talk; does it take you down or does it lift you? Stop judging yourself; do a detox where you don't complain about what happened for a week and see how you feel.

We have to stop thinking less of ourselves and think of ourselves more. We need to stop using the terms good or bad when we apply it to ourselves or others. We are multidimensional. We are whole people having a human experience. On some days we will have healthy behaviour and on other days not so healthy, such as anger, greed, and jealousy. We all do things that are wrong and fail. Watch how you define yourself. Also don't take on other people's labels. If you act in a way that is not healthy, forgive yourself, learn from it and move on.

Shadow self

Carl Jung identified that people have shadows which they disown. The shadow represents things we can't see in ourselves. Our shadows are in our subconscious, and we need to bring them to our conscious. We need to be aware of our shadow. We often see the shadow in others but not in ourselves. We need to own our shadow and flaws, have awareness and give ourselves compassion. If we try to reward our shadow in positive ways, this will help us stop using negative ways, i.e., accept our shadows and bring them into our lives. Our shadows have needs that need to meet, i.e., like needing attention or wanting control.

"Although many infer the shadow is 'negative', this is not really true. The Shadow is rather what you yourself perceive as dark and weak about yourself, and therefore needing to be hidden and denied".[42]

When something goes wrong, people are uncomfortable and embarrassed and often project the blame on someone else. We all fall short in life, not one of us is perfect. If we deny these in ourselves but we can see in others, we project them onto others to bury ours.

If we get triggered by someone, it is often our shadow. Usually when an emotion comes up, it is from a shadow. We need to integrate our shadow within ourselves. This means owning it. For me one of my shadows is recognition/significance where I have a need to be recognised for the work I do. During the bullying experience, this need was not met by others. However, it is my responsibility to feed my shadow in a positive way and not rely on other people to do so.

Often bullies are projecting their insecurities onto other people.

---

[42] Jacobson, Sheri. Your 'Shadow' Self – What It Is, And How It Can Help You, harleytherapy.com, https://www.harleytherapy.co.uk/counselling/shadow-self.htm., September 7, 2017

*Your task is not to seek for love,
but merely to seek and find all the
barriers within yourself that you
have built against it*
—Rumi.

Taking back your power

I went through a lot with gaslighting and the subtle suggestions that my thoughts were wrong leaving me with the conclusion I was wrong or the way I was wrong. I felt I could no longer bring myself to work, all of me, warts and all. The indication to me through the gaslighting was who I was, was not acceptable to them. I was tired of trying to contort myself into who they thought I should be and why should I do that. It was of no benefit to me and my soul. The effort to define me, I reject. I am no longer allowing other people to define me and tell me who I am. I am who God created me to be.

Too often we allow our income and our employer's wants to determine us, our work, and our value. We live in fear of not having an income, so we sacrifice ourselves to the money altar instead of looking after ourselves and our own happiness. We have also been trained to think that having a job is the only way to go in life to earn money. There other options, like becoming an entrepreneur.

We need to recognise we have the power to make decisions and the power to leave situations. We can't remain the victim of this situation forever. We have to move on to joy and thriving and leave this situation behind. Let it go and surrender.

We can't allow the other person to have power over us even when we are in fear.

We need to recognise we have the power over what thoughts we allow in our brain. We have to choose to change our thoughts and our identity. We are survivors and we can move on and create an amazing life for ourselves. We have to believe that life can change, and we can be our own creators.

You set the standard for how people treat you. Decide on how you want to be treated and let people know.

> *You teach people how to treat you by what you allow, what you stop, and what you reinforce*—A. Gaskins Jr.

Boundaries

> *How people treat you is their karma; how you react is yours. With everything that has happened to you, you can either feel sorry for yourself or treat what has happened as a gift. Everything is either an opportunity to grow or an obstacle to keep you from growing. You get to choose*—Wayne W. Dyer.

There are many different types of boundaries: physical, mental, emotional, sexual, financial, intellectual, and material.

There are two types of people with poor boundaries, and these are:

- People who take responsibilities for everyone
- People who expect others to take on their responsibilities

Having healthy boundaries means:

- You can say no
- And you can accept no from others

Boundaries were a really big issue for me as I found that I let other people walk over me as I was a people pleaser. In some circumstances, I could put a boundary in and other times I had none. I learned the hard way how important it is to value yourself and put boundaries in. As part of this is being able to ask for what you want and being able to say NO, if you don't want to do something it is okay to say NO. Don't give an explanation as to why as this creates more issues. Choose what you want to do. People often refer to NO as a complete sentence.

One of the main boundaries is letting people know that their behaviour is unacceptable. How do you do that in a powerful way that delivers the message and tells the other person about what behaviour you expect from them in a compassionate way? Sometimes you can give the feedback immediately and at other times, it will take planning and working out what to say. Sometimes you can let it go because it was a one-off event and you won't ever deal with them again.

There are a few methods of dealing with other people's behaviour. One method is the "I feel" where you say things like, I feel that you are not listening to me, etc. At no time should you attack them with anger. Other methods include stating what their behaviour was, how it affected you, what you want from them going forward.

However, at the end of it there is no guarantee the other person is going to listen and take action on their behaviour. In most cases, people are reasonable and take it on board.

Wanting to look after your own needs is not selfish. You need to give yourself sleep, health foods, mind breaks, being on your own, and having time out for yourself. Only you know what your body and mind need; please honour them.

Boundaries and people with toxic behaviour

Unfortunately, with people with toxic behaviour, it is likely that they will not respect your boundaries and will repeatedly violate them.

These people are ones that:

- Don't respect your boundaries
- Take advantage of your kindness
- Use manipulation to get what they want
- Don't consider your feelings
- Put you down
- Often, they will say what they want but will not listen to you

Usually there is no reasonable discussion that can be taken. Sometimes these people will never respect your boundaries, but you can still put some in and reinforce them. You will have to learn to be strong and call out their crap and when they learn that they can't manipulate you, they will likely move onto another target.

There are some ways to deal with this:

- Ask for what you want but don't go into explanations or defend yourself
- Going no contact, i.e., leaving your job
- Practise detachment on the outcome
- Learn to heal your triggers so you don't react to them

Learning to face obstacles and challenges

Life's challenges are not supposed to paralyze you, they're supposed to help you discover who you are
—Bernice Johnson Reagon.

Obstacles and challenges are here to help us grow. Throughout life we will encounter obstacles and challenges and how we deal with them is important. The best way to deal with these is to tackle them face on as they are not going away.

With the obstacles and challenges come the lessons you need to learn to face them.

And once the storm is over, you won't remember how you made it through, how you managed to survive. You won't even be sure whether the storm is really over. But one thing is certain. When you come out of the storm, you won't be the same person who walked in. That's what this storm's all about—Haruki Murakami.

Belief

"Beliefs can be described as views we have about ourselves, others and the world as a whole. They determine how we think things are and how they are supposed to be. In fact, how we see the world is determined by what we have decided to believe about it.

The sum of our beliefs, both positive ones and negative ones make up our mindset and thus our idea of reality. Everything in life, from how we see things, how we feel about them and how we react to them is determined by our subconscious belief system which is at the core of who we are.[43]

Beliefs that we have developed from childhood hold us back from living our lives. These beliefs are wired into our subconscious. Some of these beliefs are:

- I am not good enough
- I will be happy when, i.e., a particular event will happen
- Loving myself is selfish
- I will be judged if I show my real self
- I don't have any value
- I am not worthy
- What I offer no one will pay for

We also allow our current circumstances to hold us back and we think this is the only way we know how to live, and nothing will change. These beliefs hold us back from allowing good things to happen in our lives. Our beliefs can be affected by our emotions and feelings, and these can be very strong, and we don't look at things rationally or logically. In addition, we have a confirmation bias where if we believe something, we look for evidence to prove it is true. Our beliefs can lie to us and sometimes we believe in the authority of institutions and accept what they tell us. Our beliefs can exist to help us promote our self-interest.

Somehow over time I developed a belief that I could not do the things other people could and that I was not worthy or could expect good things to happen to me. Life became a struggle with reacting to what was being presented to me.

---

[43] Huber, Liz. Why Limiting Beliefs Hold You Back in Life & What To Do About It The Invisible Walls Between You and Your Dreams, medium.com, https://medium.com/swlh/why-limiting-beliefs-hold-you-back-in-life-what-to-do-about-it-e877f6e36bd2

Those messages kept on coming, so did the abuse from others and from myself. Messages of being broken, not good for anyone. I did not expect anything. I did not want to receive or thought I could receive. All the gifts that were there from heaven were refused and laid unopened. I did not believe I could own a house or be happy.

Not believing really holds you back from achieving or expecting things in life. This you can change by altering your thoughts. Choosing your thoughts is important. We have the power to change our beliefs and thoughts. I had to make a choice that I wanted life to be different, one that is not so crappy or without joy. It took me a long time to realise I could make this choice; it took a really bad experience with ill health and gaslighting and bullying to get me to quit one of my jobs. I gave so much to my job and other people, and they took what I offered. There were good relationships where I worked, and those ones were win/win. Now it is time to give all that to myself so I can then give out from a full cup instead of an empty one.

I can now choose a life of joy and believing in myself. The mind shift from employee and entrepreneur has been a hard journey. I was struggling to believe that I can make money from this, but this is my only choice and I have to give it a go otherwise I will really regret it. I don't want to go back to the old life where I had little joy or allowed myself to be treated badly. I have worked over a number of months changing my money mindset to believing in myself and making an income as an entrepreneur.

Little steps

Take any changes in your life slowly, step by step. Changing habits takes time for them to stick. You can learn to change one habit for another one and this will help. A good idea is to track your habits.

Divide your goal into little steps because sometimes the goal becomes too overwhelming and then you don't get started or you stop it completely as it becomes too hard.

Find the next little step and complete it and then do the next step and over a year you will be surprised how much you have achieved. Sometimes the steps could be as simple as write one paragraph or exercise for five minutes. Once you get started the steps can become bigger.

If you stop or find the step too big, break it down until you feel able to complete the next step.

*Stop wasting your time on people who make you feel like a completely different person that you hardly recognize.
Find the people that encourage you to be not only yourself, but to be the BEST version of yourself.
Remember: Nobody is worth losing yourself over*—Mel Robbins.

Life after

When the trauma is so real
The body and mind are hurting with pain
The letting go comes first
The healing takes it time
The slow steps start with forgiving ourselves
Then adding in those things that give us joy
Allowing ourselves to just be
As the creative spark prepares to unleash
The trauma ceases to be
As the life after begins

Elizabeth Gray 2020

Chapter 14

Learning From Experiences

Bullying is a horrible thing. It sticks with you forever. It poisons you. But only if you let it
—Heather Brewer.

How do I look at my experiences of being bullied and gaslighted? With all experiences, there is a positive and a negative. For a long time, I believed things were happening to me rather than for me. I had settled with accepting mistreatment from others, but I still underneath wanted a lot more of life. I made a decision that I wanted a different life. I also had a number of coaches that helped me move from the victim to survivor and to have more control over my life. To come out of a fairly traumatic experience I was more determined than ever to create the life I wanted. I made a number of decisions for my life: not to live my life in fear, to be healthy, to do what I love, to be my best, best I can be, and follow my purpose. I have come out valuing myself and knowing my worth and it is not defined by other people.

One thing I learned was I was addicted to my old story as a victim, and I had woven it into my life so much it was a part of me. I found it near impossible to change. The old story was who I had become, and I allowed myself to be trapped in this story as it was the only story I knew. Once I understood this concept of my story and its impact on me, I wrote out my old story and I could see it was told from a victim point of view and then I wrote out a new story of who I wanted to be. Knowing I could change my story was powerful and one where I was living a life of joy and thriving.

We have all created particular identities into our lives, such as employee, manager, husband, wife, mother, father, son, daughter, accountant, sales assistant, chief financial officer, director, celebrity, etc. These help us identify who we are. If we lose these suddenly, like quitting a job after bullying, we have lost our previous identity as an employee and grieve. But ultimately, you can create a new identity for yourself.

We have created these identities that are stuck in the past. We focus on our reality and it looks like we are not successful, or we are failures because we feel things have not changed for us and we feel stuck. Failure is an event; it is not us personally. It is okay to have failures, this is part of life. **Rejection is redirection**. We need to change our perception and believe in the future even if we can't see it. We can create our own future.

How would you like to write a new story about yourself? That you are empowered, full of love and kindness. Who are you? Write out your new story, what your perfect day is, where you would like to live, what you want to be doing every day, what time of income you want. Once you write it out, keeping reading it every day.

The past, or what happened to you, does not define your future. The key here is believing and creating your future.

Reality vs future

Thoughts of your mind have made you what you are and thoughts of your mind will make you what you become from this day forward—**Catherine Ponder.**

Often, we get stuck in our reality of what is happening now rather than our future. We don't think that anything will change for us and that we don't deserve any more. We allow our reality to influence our future. We can create our future from current circumstances and not from what might happen if we took the risk to move forward. Our future is determined by our actions, beliefs, and thoughts. We have to stop giving other people power of our lives and how we see them. We can break out of the mould and believe and do things differently and create a life for ourselves. No life will be without challenges, and we have to learn how to embrace them and deal with them.

Dr. Joe Dispenza talks about feeling what we want our life in the future to be and believing we already have it. "The best way to predict the future is to create it, not from the known but from the unknown. Close your eyes and think about that vision of your future. Once you start thinking about it, you're activating the creative centers in your brain. Naturally, you begin to think about putting yourself in the scene of your future. The act of doing this when you're truly present and passionate is shaping a new destiny for you. The moment you're defined by that vision, and the thoughts in your mind become the experience, you begin to feel the emotions of the future before their made manifest. Get ready, because when you do this daily you're changing every aspect of who you currently are."[44]

For example, imagine the house you are living in is your dream house every day for a few minutes. You can do this with your ideal car, ideal business, ideal partner. Keep on doing this and believing.

---

[44] Dizpensa, Dr Joe. Dr Joe Dispenza - OFFICIAL NEWS & FAN PAGE https://www.facebook.com/DrJoeDispenzaOfficialNewsFanPage/posts/the-best-way-to-predict-the-future-is-to-create-it-not-from-the-known-but-from-t/3454293341262702/, August 8, 2019

Being grateful

> *Rejection is merely a redirection; a course correction to your destiny*—Bryant McGill.

Forgiveness and surrender are very important steps but being grateful for the situation removes the sting from what happened. The event and what happened sucks but there are so many silver linings and wisdom from what happened to us from these experiences. These experiences are sent to help us grow and develop to who we are meant to be. Either we ignore them, and they keep coming back louder and louder and a major event happens in our lives, or we meet them head on. Tapping into being grateful means we can see what has benefited us from these events and we would not have grown and become who we are without them.

My value/silver linings are:

- Rejection is redirection. Sometimes when we get rejected, we are being redirected to do something else and that can be amazing and better than what we had before
- I am now on my journey to fulfilling my purpose in life and had I stayed working I wouldn't be on this journey
- I no longer allow people and what they say about me to define me
- I am listening to my intuition more and more and it is leading me to where God wants me to be
- I know how valuable I am and what I have to offer
- I am now more prepared to ask for help when I need it, instead of trying to things by myself
- I am now having the courage to chase what I love to do with my writing
- I am facing my fears and working through them

- I have found a supportive tribe that builds me and does not tear me down
- Being able to let the criticism wash over more than in the past
- I know that I am not broken and there is nothing wrong with me
- Really accepting and knowing my authentic self
- Putting boundaries around myself is very important
- Saying yes to myself first so when I serve I do it from a full cup

I found it very powerful for my healing to write a letter to the person that bullied me (**don't send it to them**) and thanking them for what I learned from this experience. You can tear up or destroy the letter after writing.

Asking for help and what I needed

Growing up I was never taught to ask for what I want and what I needed. I was just expected to just take the crumbs and if I gave and gave and others took and took from me that was okay. However, this is not okay; there needs to be a balance in life between giving and receiving as they are part of the same thing. Part of another issue I faced with my life was the fact I didn't know how to receive; I didn't know how to get the good things in life or believe they would come for me. I had a lot of issues from not feeling worthy or of being rejected, having self-doubt, having no confidence, being afraid of success, and being afraid of failure.

For years I didn't expect anything good to come to me. I didn't expect to receive really nice things and a lot of my interactions were very negative because my vibration was low. People thought they could take from me because my vibration was low. It was put onto me that I needed to take responsibility for others, but their stuff did not belong to me, and they needed to take responsibility for it.

Often with trauma, people become very independent and don't ask for help as trust is broken. Independence is often valued as a strength, but it prevents us from becoming strong by asking for help. If independence is part of your survival, then it can do you more damage. Bullying can cause people to go within and become independent. We need to gather trust again and build relationships.

Asking for help is okay and normal and you will be very surprised when you discover there are lots of people out there that want to help you.

Giving and receiving

> *Giving is only one-half of the law of increase. Receiving is the other half. We can give and give but we may unbalance the law unless we also expect to receive*—**Catherine Ponder.**

Too often we are taught to give and give but we are not taught to receive. Imagine receiving a compliment on what you are wearing. Do you accept it, or do you shrug it off and give an explanation that this old thing is 10 years old? Giving and receiving go together. Allowing others to give to you is wonderful. We need to open ourselves up. For way too long, I did not allow myself to receive. I was taught to give. I also believed that I was unworthy to receive. This prevented me from receiving from others and from God. There are a few wonderful resources out there on receiving—*The Art of Receiving* by Amanda Owen, *It's Not Your Money* by Tosha Silver, and Catherine Ponder's work.

My role given to me by God is to shine my light and tell my story. Also, why not me? Why can't I receive blessings that others are receiving? Others can do this entrepreneurial journey, so can I. It may not feel safe or it is beyond my comfort zone but the old comfort zone of employment where I am abused and treated so badly is pain and suffering and is worse than taking the risk. I am trusting you, God, with this journey into the scary future space, but I know it will be okay. It will be back and forward scary, safe, scary, safe, but you are with me on this journey. I am trusting in you, God.

You are worthy of having great goals and moving towards them. Why not you? This is the start of believing that you are worthy of your goals and dreams. You are deserving of these as much as anyone else is. So, start changing your beliefs and thoughts. You can do this through journaling or affirmations.

Resilience

> *"God is faithful, and he will not let you be tested beyond your strength but with your testing he will also provide the way out so that you may be able to endure it"*
> **1 Corinthians 10:13**[45]

When I look back on all my experiences and how I survived them, I realised I have resilience. I was like a palm tree able to bend with the wind. I am stronger than I thought. Despite all that was thrown at me, I survived, and I grew through the experiences. Being able to be adaptable and having the core belief inside that I don't deserve this treatment kept me going.

---

[45] Biblica, Inc. TM, The Holy Bible, New International Version® NIV®

Somewhere deep inside my soul was a voice saying enough is enough and I was able to come up and work and survive. I know God gave me strength to get through what had happened to me. Coming out of the healing process I know that I can cope with changes and what is thrown at me. I may pause or stop but I will restart and keep on going.

> *Resilience is accepting your new reality, even if it's less good than the one you had before. You can fight it, you can do nothing but scream about what you've lost, or you can accept that and try to put together something that's good*—Elizabeth Edwards.

Moving from victim to survivor

As we go through the journey, we have to move from victim to survivor. Being a victim is where we start but it is not where we have to end. Remaining a victim means we are stuck in the thinking and emotional mud pit. I remember being told stop being a victim but never being told how to stop being a victim. Stop being a victim means taking fully responsibility for yourself and your response to other people.

Things you can do include:

- Having no self-judgement
- Prioritise yourself
- Learn to love yourself
- Stop wanting other people's approval

Watch your language in the way you refer to yourself and your circumstances.

Example: Life sucks
Victim: Life sucks, all the bad things seem to happen to me
Survivor: Life may suck but I can look at things in a different way and work on my future

Example: I am a bad person
Victim: I am the bad person and I can't do anything right
Survivor: I am neither a good or bad person and although I make mistakes, I do good things

Example: Nobody loves me
Victim: I am not worthy; I don't have any value and nobody loves me
Survivor: I am worthy of love; I have lots of friends and I am open to love

> ***Life is about accepting the challenges along the way, choosing to keep moving forward, and savoring the journey*—Roy T. Bennett**

Celebrating our wins

Too often we focus on what went wrong and we forget the wins we have had in life. It is good to keep a journal of our wins and regularly celebrate them as they happen. You can celebrate by dancing around the house, a walk by the beach, buying yourself flowers or a book, an inspirational card, or having a simple meal.

Read over your wins journal often and this will remind you of all the things you have achieved.

There is no greater thing you can do with your life and your work than follow your passions – in a way that serves the world and you
—Richard Branson.

Healing Myself

The layers of trauma
In my life
Are beginning to unravel
And become more exposed
Feeling the pain
And tears swelling up
But knowing these are
Coming up
So, I can heal them
And learn from them
Acknowledge their silver linings
And how these experiences
Have helped me grow
Into who I am today
Showing up for myself
With courage
And knowing
Healing myself
Is the best gift I can give
Myself

Elizabeth Gray 2021

Chapter 15

How We Know When We Are Healed

And the day came when the risk to remain tight in a bud was more painful than the risk it took to blossom—Anaïs Nin.

One of the ways we know we are on the way to healing is when we don't think about what happened to us anymore and we become excited about our future and moving forward. There is no longer a pull about what has happened and/or the feeling of anger and having the thought of vengeance. I find when I can forgive a person and send them love, I know I have moved on. Sometimes the memories do come back, and I have to practise this again.

We can see the silver lining about what this situation is about and learn and move on. The situation will give you many blessings. For me, I am grateful for the experiences as I am able to live a different life from before and I appreciate and value myself. I understand that I have a purpose to help others.

Give yourself time to heal and don't hurry it or judge yourself. The first time where I was shaken to my core, it took nearly two years to heal and the second major incident around 12 months. I also did a lot of work on my mindset and healing my inner child. Some of our triggers are unhealed things that went on when we were younger. Some of things I needed to look at was joining my feminine with my masculine. For too long, there was a divide within me; I had disconnected from myself as this was the only way to push through and manage the pain. The masculine is more about the doing and giving while the feminine is receiving and being in the flow. At corporate workplaces, usually the masculine is dominant, and we are valued in the workplace for doing.

Take time out and create a new identity where you see yourself as worthy and your own hero and not as the victim. You can change your life by choosing to do so. Yes, it is hard work, but it is worth it.

Counteracting bullying

The best way to counteract bullying is to really love your worth and know your worth and not take on what is being said about you. Put in boundaries over their behaviour. You are being attacked by the bullies due to their insecurities about themselves and they feel threatened by you.

Please love yourself as you are so worthy. Ask good friends what they love about you. You matter. Have confidence in your abilities.

Know your truth of who you are.

Part Five
Life After Bullying

The best way to predict your future is to create it—Abraham Lincoln.

Finding My Voice

For too long the voice inside has been silent
Made to be so small
In order to keep it safe
To try not upset anyone else
Every time it tried to speak up
Someone made a comment
And it was pushed down again
One day everything came to be too much
The unhappiness was there all the time
Who decided that my voice was unworthy?
Why did I allow those voices to drown out my own?
Everyone has a voice
Everyone has been given a gift
Little by little the voice has been speaking
Starting in whispers
Raising louder and louder
Speaking truth, authenticity and from vulnerability
Being truth to itself
Following the intuition
To expand and grow
And to be the voice that is required
To change things in the world

Elizabeth Gray 2020

Chapter 16

Big Dreams and Life After Bullying

Every day think as you wake up, today I am fortunate to be alive, I have a precious human life, I am not going to waste it. I am going to use all my energies to develop myself, to expand my heart out to others; to achieve enlightenment for the benefit of all beings. I am going to have kind thoughts towards others, I am not going to get angry or think badly about others. I am going to benefit others as much as I can—The Dalai Lama.

Don't downgrade your dream just to fit your reality. Upgrade your conviction to match your destiny—@empoweringwomannow.com

What impact and legacy do you want to leave the world? Do you want to leave one of negativity or positivity?

You are the creator of your life and not the people that bullied you. You are so powerful and can create an amazing life for yourself. Believe in it. You can do it. No one has the right to define you.

We have so much power in us to create our reality and different lives for ourselves. We react to our circumstances and allow these to dictate what happens in the future. We allow the ways we understand and live, and we don't open the possibility to other things. The things that we should do are the work we love and to create joy and fun in our lives. I know in the past I have stopped myself having fun and joy as the old belief has held me back that I need to suffer in my work, but I don't need to believe that anymore. Some of the simple things like buying flowers, walking by the beach, buying a special treat, going to the art gallery, spending time on craft or painting, or catching up with friends and sitting quietly in the park. We need to dedicate more time to having joy and doing things we can fill ourselves up with.

Doing little changes every day can change our lives and beliefs and create a new life for ourselves. Let's dream big. Putting in the effort until we are successful. Too often we find things hard, and we give up rather than push through and take a risk. For me writing this book and putting it into the world is a risk. It might fail and not go anywhere but it also might take off and really help people. The most important thing was finishing this book and the journey I went on to get there. I have grown so much while writing this book; I am healing and creating a new future for myself. I would have never imagined how I could do this. I have to stop focusing on the destinations and realise the journey is the most important thing to do. We change as we go along the journey, and it is not a straight-line journey, it is up and down.

For far too long, I did not believe in my dreams, and this stopped me from working on them and persisting until I saw success. Now, I need to work towards my dream and will love who I will become along the way. By staying comfortable, we are risking our lives and our happiness and joy. Too often comfort is what we accept; and this means we stay in abusive relationships, whether it is personal or in your workplace. Saying yes to our goals and dreams means we change ourselves and that can inspire others to do the same. Also, we can help people along the way and help them achieve their dreams. It does hurt your life by staying comfortable. There is no growth, and everything remains the same and you are not fulfilled. I don't want to regret in another 5 or 10 years that I did not take the risk to follow my dreams.

Place lots of trust in God. I did. I know he is directing my journey.

> *Shoot for the moon. Even if you miss, you'll land among the stars*—Les Brown.

Finding your voice

It is important to find your voice and speak up and ask for what you want. It is okay to express your needs. It is also good to be vulnerable and let others know where we are at. Instead of saying we are okay, we can say that we are struggling. For me it is telling people I have been depressed or am feeling overwhelmed. Everyone has a unique voice, and everyone matters.

Part of writing this book was about me finding my voice and not being silent anymore. Too often the shame about being bullied will keep us silent. The fear from the bully also makes us more silent as we know how much damage they can do to us. Become brave and face your fear of the bully and don't give them power over you. Also, if you are the first speaking up about a bullying incident, it is so hard as so often you are not being believed. Speaking up for yourself will help you heal. It might be voicing to friends or health professionals to help you move on.

Look how the world has changed with people speaking up. In Australia, so many women are coming forward and speaking about their experiences with sexual abuse. Marches are being held because want a different world. Speaking up has to start somewhere and this is the way we can get things changed.

Divine purpose listening to your soul and the messages

We are built for a purpose and we need to listen to our heart and follow it. Our soul does give us messages all the time on what we are supposed to do. But over time we have been taught to follow the logic and ignore the soul. The heart leads you to where you should be. Being in the vibration of love is so powerful. Sometimes you get a feeling on what you should do and then you dismiss it. Not all feelings are correct but when it feels peaceful and knowing and there is no fear around it, you should consider following this guidance. Inside of us is our inner guidance system planted by God.

Nobody else but you is designed for a specific purpose and God can't get his role done without you fulfilling your purpose. You might think it's too late; you might think you are too young. Whatever it is, it's all being worked out by God. Everyone has something to offer and if you look back and you look at your friends and it's most likely that they have made a difference in your life. You don't know how you have touched people's lives by encouraging friends, smiling or talking to a stranger, or helping someone. You don't have to be big in the world on a giant stage to make a difference. So, don't ever underestimate, your ability with a kind word, a smile, a gift, a gesture; it is the most beautiful gift you can give to the world.

God has given me a blessing, and no one can knock me out of this.

Whatever's meant to happen, will happen; And everything that has happened, happened for a reason—Margaret Skipper.

Be brave
Take a chance
Do something towards
Those wonderful goals
That will bring joy
And beauty in your life

Doing the things for yourself that you love

It is important that you do things you love, i.e., walks by the water and ocean or forest, crafting, gardening, fishing, time with family, cooking. Find the things you enjoy. It is okay to look after yourself. This is really important that you do the things you love. I used to block myself off doing things as I felt guilty as there was so much to be done in my house. We are also taught to feel guilty doing things for ourselves. But fill your cup first. I used to do an hour every day on my quilting project or some painting.

Timetable the time in; you will feel a lot better doing the things that bring joy into your life. Quite often we are conscious of this and sabotage ourselves and don't feel worthy or feel that it is self-indulgent. I find it hard sometimes to do this myself. I feel I should be working but doing the things I love fires me up.

Do the things that expand you.

Find your tribe

The best thing you can do is gather your tribe around you. You need people that support you and encourage you so that you can achieve what you want. You want the people around that see what you are capable of doing even if you can't see it in yourself.

If you need help from health professionals, find those who you are comfortable in talking with and being open.

The most important gift that you can ever give yourself is to be yourself, to be what you were created to be; just find that voice and get out there and just be who you truly were meant to be, free from societal expectations, just really listen within.

Moving into the future ensuring no repeating

Focus on the future. Too often we let the past and what happened to us stop us going into the future. We can change our future and not let ourselves be defined by the past. This means we need to learn our lessons of what this episode in our life was teaching us.

Some things I am thankful for my experience are:

- I know now that I am valuable and worthy of so much more
- I am no longer working in workplaces where I am not appreciated
- I have a wonderful opportunity to be healthy and pursue my passions and my purpose
- Thank you for teaching me around boundaries and that I will no longer tolerate bad behaviour

Contribution forward

What contribution will you make? Our purpose on this planet is to serve others. Even if you only help one person you make a difference in this world. Imagine how many people you can help through sharing your story and what happened to you. Too often we view our contribution as nothing. So, imagine you are having a bad day, and someone smiles at you. Do you think that would lift you up?

Do you think someone's story about sexual abuse would help you if you had one? Do you think my story about being bullied in the workplace will help someone? I do hope so as I have felt compelled that I need to share this story so people know you can move on from bullying. It is important that we are not held back by the bullies in our lives. We can heal and move on with our lives. The lessons we learn are so important to our growth and our purpose. There is always a silver lining with what happens in our lives. There is always a positive and negative from events in our lives. The aim is to make them neutral so that they don't trigger us anymore.

Looking back at the situations I went through; I am grateful that they gave me so much growth and put me on the path that I was meant to take. The difficulties made me stronger and more resilient and made me realise that I don't want to accept bad behaviour from people in my private or work life. I want to be surrounded by a tribe of people that can see the good in me and help me improve and do better. I want to be supported and not torn down by people. There will always be misunderstandings, failures, and mistakes in relationships but that is okay, I will learn from them as well.

My aim is to become a better person each day as I held myself back far too long from being who I was meant to be. As I have gone through this journey and book I have changed and grown into myself. I finally feel at home with me and what I have to offer. People can take that or leave it as I will not appeal to everyone. If I challenge you, can I ask you to look at your own stories and decide what is being triggered.

Dream big

Do you remember your dreams as a child? What did you want to be? As a young child, I wanted to be an actress or model; this did later change to artist and writer. Write down your ideal life, how you want to spend your day, where you would live, who you would be with, what you would wear, what you would eat. Read this ideal life every day to yourself.

Imagine how you want that to be. Do you think you can achieve it? Stop there before you answer. Lots of things are possible in this world. Shoot for the moon. If you can't imagine a future life for yourself, you are downgrading and playing small.

What future did you imagine for yourself?

Is it time to move forward and claim it for yourself? Whether or not you make the destination it is about the journey and who you become on the journey.

Be committed

When we do things, we need to be committed to them until we are successful. I mean really committed. Without commitment, it is easy to give up. There will be setbacks along the way and times when you want to give up. Often, we have not pushed through and tried enough to succeed. Sometimes we convince ourselves that our goal is not possible, but we really need to believe and be determined to achieve our goals and dreams.

If you have trouble committing to yourself and dreams, please get a coach or someone that can make you accountable. External accountability is easier to get things done but internal accountability is better. Using your dreams and goals to inspire you so that you want to get up and do it and keep yourself accountable.

Keep practising and moving forward to achieve what you want.

Keep promises to yourself

The most important person to keep your promises to is yourself—Unknown.

It is important to make small promises to yourself and keep them. These are small things but important. Often the person we let the most down is ourselves and we break our promises to ourselves. We must keep small, important promises to ourselves.

Not all storms come to disrupt your life, some come to clear your path
—Unknown.

One Wild and Precious Life

My one wild and precious life
I only have one
To live fully present
To learn about myself
To be myself
Discover my beauty within
Bring joy to others and myself
Follow my heart
To pursue my purpose
And passion
To do what I love
While serving others
There is no other way
To live fully
And enjoy the precious gift
Of my life

Elizabeth Gray 2020

Conclusion

One Wild and Precious Life

I love Mary Oliver's quote; this is from her poem "The Summer Day."

> *"Tell me, what is it you plan to do*
> *With your one wild and precious life?"*

We need to treat our lives as precious and do more with it. We all should be flourishing but somehow, we have been told that it is hard, we have to sacrifice and not be happy.

I am meant to be joyful, serving others with my specific purpose. Not a life of suffering. There will be down days but that is okay as it provides contrast in my life.

Coming home to me being happy in my skin and who I am and that I define me, no one else. It is such a happy place to be in. Despite the ups and downs. I am home at last.

At the end is information regarding what I believe workplaces should be doing to counteract bullying and narcissistic behaviour in the workplace as the current situation is not working. I know so many people that have been at the end of this behaviour.

Those that have suffered, I hope this helps you on your journey to healing.

> *The more you are motivated by love,*
> *the more fearless and free your action*
> *will be*—Dalai Lama.

I hope telling my story will help others through their journey with toxic workplaces. You do not have to be defined by these

Elizabeth Gray

experiences. You are worthy of so much more. You don't have to live that. You can be your own hero and live a life you want. Finding your own voice is so important and what you say matters. Live your one wild and precious life.

I am on my journey and moving forward with my life. Part of my healing journey is finding my voice, standing up and speaking up that bullying and toxic behaviour is not acceptable and that it should not be allowed to continue to workplaces. Writing my poetry and this book has been part of my healing journey. I am not all the way through, but I am hopeful of my future, one I get to create.

I have added in exercises and resources for those who want to do some inner work or get help. Working through the fear is the hardest as is acknowledging you need help.

Part Six
References and Help

At the end of the day people won't remember what you said or did, they will remember how you made them feel—Maya Angelou.

Remaining Open

Remaining open
Being vulnerable
And authentic
As I tell my story
Allow yourself the listener
To be uncomfortable
And put yourself in my shoes
It does not matter if you disagree
But have empathy and compassion
As we all have issues in our hearts
That have given us wounds
Allow us to speak
As this helps healing to occur
Don't minimise or trivialise
What I say
Because you don't understand
Or use it for political purposes
Or for your own agenda
Hearing others is important
Acknowledge them
Nothing can be resolved
Unless listening and understanding
Is there
Be the person that wants to be
Part of the solution

Elizabeth Gray 2021

Workplace Bullying—What Employers Need To Do

Compassion is not religious business, it is human business, it is not luxury, it is essential for our own peace and mental stability, it is essential for human survival
—Dalai Lama.

My suggestions below are to an extent based on my experience. There are many different experiences in workplaces where there is great leadership and employees are treated well while there are other companies where employees are not treated well and there are workplaces where there is good and bad treatment. No workplace or employee is perfect as we all are human and have human experiences in the workplace.

What I want out of this chapter is to show how things can be done differently to achieve the results and profits in the business without resorting to bullying behaviour. We need to value that everyone is in a different space and the solution is really listening to people and validating what they say even if we disagree with what they are saying.

Pressures do build up in workplaces as there are so many stresses and I am advocating to take time out and listen to your employees. See if you can do anything differently. A lot of disputes between employees are due to lack of listening and giving understanding. Adverse opinions should be welcomed as should solutions to the issues. The aim should be to find common ground between employees. Employees all have different backgrounds, cultures, and beliefs and helping them to succeed in their work and life brings so many gifts to a workplace.

How do you want your employees to feel?

How do you want your customers to feel after having an interaction with you? You want them to feel good, so they buy again or recommend your company to someone else to buy.

How do you want your employees to feel working in your company? Do you want them to feel happy or do you not care? If your staff have a problem, do you truly listen and understand what the issue is and try to solve the problem?

Often there are procedures and processes on how things are to be handled but how are they implemented? Sometimes the care and empathy can be lost from the process.

Richard Branson's philosophy is "Take care of your employees, and they'll take care of your business."

> *I have always believed that the way you treat your employees is the way they will treat your customers, and that people flourish when they are praised*—**Richard Branson.**

Factors that contribute to workplace bullying

"Without the work environment giving the green light, providing the license to unbridled mistreatment, bullying wouldn't happen."[46]

There are a number of factors that can contribute to workplace bullying. Some of these are:

---

[46] Ziv, Stav. Don't Let Workplace Bullies Win—Here's How to Spot Them and Stop Them, themuse.com, https://www.themuse.com/advice/how-to-deal-with-workplace-bullies

- Leadership styles include autocratic which is directive and strict. This can include abusive and demeaning behaviour
- Work stressors including job insecurity
- Poorly defined roles
- Lack respectful relationships in the workplace
- Poor communication
- Bad work environment where bullying behaviour is tolerated

Even if the bullying is not substantiated, there is still a problem that needs to be solved via mediation, counselling, or changing work arrangements. It is not enough to say there is no proof and therefore it did not happen or you don't think it is bullying. It is best to be proactive, recognise there is a problem, and fix it. Why should a person lose their job because of one person's behaviour?

What can help is receiving feedback from workers on a regular basis.

Speaking up

Are your staff too scared to tell their manager when they make a mistake? A company is partially blind if staff don't feel free to speak up about things that are wrong and need to be fixed.

Speaking up needs to be normalised so people don't feel threatened that they could lose their jobs or have their reputations damaged. Speaking up allows employees to point out errors made, projects that won't work, illegal and unethical behaviour, bullying, things that have gone wrong. Do your employees feel safe to talk up? Do you respect it? You don't have to agree but listen to each other. One of the best managers I had spoke to me about their decision. I had recommended an action to be taken to solve a problem. The manager thanked me for the recommendation, and then explained why they were going to take a different action. The manager respected me in the way they handled it, and this helps the employee know that they are appreciated.

Companies need to empower their employees to talk up and speak the truth even if it is uncomfortable and is a threat to the status quo. Businesses need to really listen to what their employees are saying otherwise problems in the business will be hidden. Train your managers to really listen and ask questions.

With whistleblowing programs your employees need to trust this process works and that they have anonymity and know there is not going to be any retaliation for speaking up. Assess if your employees trust the program. Do you know whether your employees feel free to speak up? Do your policies and procedures make a situation adversarial instead of allowing a person to speak up and the other side listen?

Bringing up problems should be viewed as a strength not a weakness. Without people being able to speak, projects and other things may cost companies millions of dollars as well as adverse media publicity. Everyone benefits as does the profitability of a company when people speak up.

Feedback

Feedback is important to give and receive and to be done in a healthy manner. Both employees and managers need to be taught on how to give and receive feedback. Does your company welcome feedback from employees?

Toxicity damage to companies

Toxicity and bullying are like a cancer for an organisation and this means there is low performance and some of the consequences of allowing toxic behaviour can include bankruptcy or facing massive fines. For example, Enron Corporation had falsified their financials and the company was declared bankrupt and employees also lost their pension fund as it was invested in the company. Volkswagen had a program installed on their cars to mislead customers and US authorities around emissions. Volkswagen were fined $2.8 billion for this fraud in the US.

Workplace bullying has been shown to have significant negative impacts on the business bottom line. There is evidence of increased absenteeism and presenteeism, higher rates of staff turnover and high legal costs when cases erupt. It is estimated that workplace bullying costs Australian organisations $6 – $36 billion a year. It is estimated that 5-7% of employees have experienced a bullying event in the past six months. [47]

Often bullying is dealt with on the surface level and not looked with the context of what is happening with the employees. Also, employees are not been given the skills to handle bullying situations.

> *When a flower doesn't bloom, you fix the environment in which it grows, not the flower*—Alexander Den Heijer.

When an employee works in a toxic workplace, their performance often declines. The reasons behind this need to be examined fully before blaming the employee. What has the

---

[47] Does Workplace Bullying Have Long Term Effects?, tapintosafety.com,https://tapintosafety.com.au/does-workplace-bullying-have-long-term-effects/

manager done to help with the situation? Are they too busy to train and monitor the employee until they are able to understand and complete their work correctly? Is there a manual or has a buddy been allocated to an employee to help them do their job? Yes, there will be occasions where the employee is unable to do their job, and this should be handled with compassion and empathy. Bullying causes loss of work time, brand and reputational damage, and can create a climate of abuse.

> *Everybody is a genius. But if you judge a fish by its ability to climb a tree, it will live its whole life believing that it is stupid. The question I have for you at this point of our journey together is, "What is your genius?"*—
> Albert Einstein.

How good is your conflict management?

The ability to undertake conflict management is vital for an organisation. With disputes, sometimes it only needs someone to be listened to and understood and by talking they can come up with their own idea of how to resolve it or someone can guide them to a solution. Working things out informally can help and it allows things to be sorted before they get to being formal and once being formal often people have their backs up and are upset and it makes it harder to deal with. Having a paperwork trail to prove that a company acted within the law does not detail how the employee felt and whether they were treated fairly. These need to be components of the process.

One of the ways to help managers and other employees become aware of what bullying is, is to ask them to write down a time when they were bullied and how they felt. This will help them realise the feelings associated with being bullied.

Employees feeling psychological safety

When someone is suffering from anxiety and depression at work, do they feel safe raising this? Often people will feel judged and seen as having a mental health condition. These issues are not left at the door before coming into the office. Anyone suffering from anxiety and depression can find it difficult to open up to these issues when they do not trust the workplace or their manager to support them or believe opening up will affect how they are treated in the workplace.

When there is conflict among employees and there is a meeting, have you asked the participants whether they feel psychologically safe to attend the meeting? Do they feel safe with the other participants in the room? What support have you provided them? Sometimes giving them ideas on how to deal with a situation is helpful. Don't make the meeting adversarial where it is one against one.

If dealing with a manager where a subordinate has had problems, does the manager acknowledge that they could have managed things better or listened more to the employee or understood them more, or does the manager convince them that they are right, and the employee is wrong? Also is the manager about defending themselves and not resolving the issue and meeting in the middle?

Leadership

> *If your actions inspire others to dream more, learn more, do more, and become more, you are a leader*—John Quincy Adams.

> *Management is doing things right; leadership is doing the right things*—Peter Drucker.

A lot of companies have leadership programs but how do you know it is implemented and working? The only way to know that is to ask the teams that the manager is leading. Are the staff being developed? Is there one that is being groomed to be a leader? How is the team showing up? Do other departments know what amazing work that team is doing? Leadership must also come down from the top and lead by example.

There is a big difference between having great technical skills to do the job and being a leader. How often are the leadership skills examined? Would the subordinates of the manager follow them anywhere or would they rather the manager not be their manager?

The qualities of leadership are:

- Active listening
- Self-confidence
- Care for others
- Self-discipline
- Supportive
- Accountability
- Fairness
- Humility
- Empathy
- Integrity
- Delegation
- Vision
- Self-awareness
- Communication
- Loyalty
- Empowerment
- Emotional intelligence
- Transparency
- Honesty

Win/win

Win-Win is a belief in the Third Alternative. It's not your way or my way. It's a better way, a higher way—Stephen R Covey.

In companies, there should be win/win situations where both parties, the company and the employees, both win through resolving of the issues that come up. All situations involve humans and their emotions, and this happens to all sides including managers/leaders and the employees. At any time, emotion can be high on either side or both sides. Any discussions had should consider whether an independent third party should be involved to ensure impartiality in solving the issues.

It takes so little for each party to listen to each other and be respectful and acknowledge each other's point of view. Not everyone has to agree but put yourself in the other person's shoes and come up with the intent of resolving the issue. Unresolved issues cause more issues later on. Some issues are not a quick fix and need to be fixed on a deeper level else the issues return and cause more drama in the workplace.

There is a need to recognise that an employee might not feel comfortable talking to their manager about the issues. If this is the case, then the employee needs to talk to someone they trust in the company. The quick fix is offer them counselling with the Employee Assistance Program; this may help in the short term but if there is an issue in the workplace that needs to be resolved between two people in the workplace not fixing the employee, they perceive has a problem. There needs to proactivity to solve the issue for the employee and also keep the employee's trust around the issue.

An employee may find it difficult to speak up if there is no trust with the company or their processes. Look at the process and check with the employee around the lack of trust. Usually when an employee lacks trust in a company it is because they don't believe the company will act in joint best interests of both employee and company. Often it is not about what the other person said or did but about how they made them feel. Solving the way, a person talks to another is essential. No-one looking at the issue should classify it was trivial at all as often issues can be one of multiple incidents and looking at one incident as trivial may preclude the understanding in depth of the issues to be resolved. It is important to recognise the emotion and deal with it in an empathetic and compassionate way and resolve the issues with a win/win.

Don't keep your feelings sheltered – express them. Don't every let life shut you up—Dr. Steve Marabol.

Exercises To Help Healing

Writing is a powerful exercise to help release what is going on in your mind and also to help clarify what you want.

Why you matter

Write down 100 reasons why you matter, i.e. I matter because ………………..

Societal expectations

Write down what societal expectations you follow that are not serving you.
Write down what success means for you.

Joy dates

Make a date with yourself and go and have fun and enjoy. Doing things like that speak your creativity. Plan one regularly – once a week, once a month.

Music and dancing

Have you got a music list that you can listen to and inspire yourself in the morning? Dancing around the house to music can get the mood and vibration up.

Listening to positive words

There are so many great podcasts and videos on YouTube that have positive words spoken. Put them on in the background so they go into your subconscious. This will help raise your vibration.

Journaling

Do morning pages every morning and write out your feelings. Also, when you are going through difficulties.

Celebration journal

Have a journal to celebrate all the great things you have achieved. Rereading this will see how far you have come.

Also celebrate your wins. Give yourself a treat like a joy date, buying yourself flowers, etc.

Old story/new story

Write out your old story and examine it. Do you have a lot of victim talk there?

Write out your new story of what you want to happen in your life and what your perfect day would be.

Have an alter ego like Beyoncé with Sasha Fierce. Beyoncé used an alter ego as self-distancing to give her confidence to go on stage, but she does not use this anymore. Adele also had an alter ego. An alter ego allows us to step back from the emotion and to concentrate on the big picture.

Child exercise

Think of yourself as six to eight years old. Write a letter to yourself as a six- to eight-year-old. Give yourself advice from younger you.

Exercise as 90-year-old

Imagine yourself being successful at age 90 and write yourself a letter now and say what you're doing and give them wisdom.

Also imagine you are telling schoolchildren or your grandchildren what you did and how you got there. What were the success factors? What did you do to make your dream come true?

How do you talk to yourself?

How do you talk to yourself? Are you kind or giving criticism to yourself?

Notice what words you are saying and change them; remind yourself that are you loved and valuable, breathe and take it easy on yourself.

Practise saying: I am safe, I am loved, I am protected, I am secure, I am worthy.

What messages are other people telling you or are you telling yourself?

What type of messages did people tell you or do you tell yourself?

Hate, ugly, not good, worthless, stupid, loser, idiot, hopeless, thick, grotesque, mediocre, useless, bad.

Are you telling yourself these messages? Keep on an eye of your thoughts and change them to positive ones.

What messages could you be telling yourself instead?

Loved, worthy, smart, confident, valuable, beautiful, gorgeous, deserving, divine, admirable, adored, beloved, cherished, precious, bold, astute.

Tell yourself positive things. Louise Hay has a book called *Mirror Work* and it involves talking to yourself in the mirror every day and giving yourself positive messages.

Elizabeth Gray

Accepting yourself and your body

What do you think about your body?

Do you hate your body parts?

Do you talk badly to your body?

Nobody's body is perfect and even movie stars have something they don't like about their bodies. All our bodies have been given to us to contain our soul. You need to take care of your body; it supports you, helps you breathe, keeps blood pumping, keeps you safe.

Learn to accept your body. Your body won't change or do anything unless you accept it and love it for itself where it is at this moment in time. This will help you move forward as resisting what is keeps you stuck.

Make a commitment to accept yourself and your body.

Resources

Contacts for anxiety and depression

Australia
- Beyond Blue 1300 22 4636 beyondblue.org.au
- RUOK ruok.org.au
- Lifeline 13 11 14 lifeline.org.au
- 1800RESPECT – 1800 737 732 1800respect.org.au for sexual assault, domestic or family violence and abuse
- Heads up – headsup.org.au – Better mental help in the workplace

USA
- The National Suicide Prevention Lifeline 1-800-273-8255 http://suicidepreventionlifeline.org
- 211 for emergency referrals but not life-threatening emergencies

Canada
- Canada Suicide Prevention Service -1-833-456-4566 http://www.crisisservicescanada.ca

UK
- Samaritans - 116 123 (http://www.samaritans.org)
- Phone 111, Option 2- National Health Services' First Response Service for mental health crises and support.

Resources around narcissism

Lisa A. Romano—Breakthrough Life Coach Inc on YouTube
Surviving Narcissism TV Dr Les Carter on YouTube
You Can Thrive After Narcissistic Abuse by Melanie Tonia Evans

Books

Mirror Work by Louise Hay
Taming Toxic People by David Gillespie
The Artist's Way by Julia Cameron
The Power of Receiving by Amanda Owen
It's Not Your Money by Tosha Silver

Prayer

If you need prayer, you could contact your local church.

Both organisations below offer prayer for healing.
Healing Rooms Australia—https://www.healingrooms.com.au
The Order of St Luke the Physician in Australia—osl.org.au

ABOUT THE AUTHOR

Elizabeth Gray was born in Melbourne and moved to Brisbane 20 years ago to enjoy the warmer weather. Elizabeth is a qualified CPA and recently left her corporate career after more than 20 years to focus on creating a different life for herself following her intuition.

Elizabeth has experienced bullying and gaslighting in the workplace. She is passionate about highlighting the issues including the physical, mental, and financial impacts it has on the victims. Elizabeth is available for speaking to corporates and others on the subject of workplace bullying.

To get in contact with Elizabeth, email her at liz_g@bigpond.com

THANK YOU

Without Dave Thompson and Davina Davidson and the team at Inspirational Book Writers, this book would have only existed as an idea and words on a page and would have stayed there. The support and help I have received has allowed me to bring one of my dreams to life to be a published author. Thanks so much for your encouragement and support.

I would also like to thank Alpa and Fiona for reading my first version of my book and making suggestions.

Thank you for those that read or bought this book. It means the world to me.

Notes

Notes

Notes

Notes

Notes

Notes

Notes

Notes

Notes